bristel

orf

patrons

mansplaining

salice — solace

befeif — Benefits

who's — whose

mers — costumers

appricate — appreciate

filmilar — unfamiliar

— advantages

there — their

stongly — staunchly

petually

left — lift

dyslexic

resiouly — ~~residuals~~ residuals

— pupils

scoll — scold

n person — impression

OWIN — shoo-in

woous — wounds

Carolina

SPELLBOUND

SPELLBOUND

My Life as a Dyslexic Wordsmith

PHIL HANLEY

Henry Holt and Company

New York

Henry Holt and Company
Publishers since 1866
120 Broadway
New York, New York 10271
www.henryholt.com

Photograph insert credits: Page 8, *Ooh La La* production photo, © Matthew Salacuse. All other photographs are from the author's personal collection.

Library of Congress Cataloging-in-Publication Data

Names: Hanley, Phil, author.
Title: Spellbound : my life as a dyslexic wordsmith / Phil Hanley.
Other titles: My life as a dyslexic wordsmith
Description: First edition. | New York : Henry Holt and Company, 2025.
Identifiers: LCCN 2024025454 | ISBN 9781250860156 (hardcover) |
    ISBN 9781250860163 (ebook)
Subjects: LCSH: Hanley, Phil. | Dyslexics—Canada—Biography. | Comedians—
    Canada—Biography. | Comedians—New York (State)—New York—Biography. |
    Male models—Biography. | Oshawa (Ont.)—Biography. | New York (N.Y.)—Biography.
Classification: LCC RC394.W6 H36 2025 | DDC 616.85/530092 [B]—dc23/
    eng/20241104
LC record available at https://lccn.loc.gov/2024025454

Our books may be purchased in bulk for promotional, educational, or business use. Please contact your local bookseller or the Macmillan Corporate and Premium Sales Department at (800) 221-7945, extension 5442, or by email at MacmillanSpecialMarkets@macmillan.com.

First Edition 2025

Designed by Gabriel Guma

Printed in the United States of America

10   9   8   7   6   5   4   3   2   1

For my mom

(You're about to see why)

Mama, mama, many worlds I've come

Since I first left home

—"BROKEDOWN PALACE," GRATEFUL DEAD

Contents

SPELLBOUND

1

Spellbound

I always prayed I'd wake up smart.

I grew up in the city of Oshawa, forty miles outside of Toronto. My friends' and neighbors' dads worked at the General Motors plant just outside of town, giving Oshawa the slogan the City that Motovates Canada. It was the '80s, and minivans were taking over the roads, and the men of Oshawa would go on to build GM's version, the Lumina APV, a vehicle nicknamed the Dustbuster for its boxy frame that narrowed into a pointy beak at the hood. When the NHL scouted for new talent, they recruited from my junior league team, the Oshawa Generals. I lived on a tree-lined street where kids played hockey year-round. They played in the snow. They played on concrete. I was in kindergarten and my older sister walked me the three blocks to school. I loved kindergarten. I loved my friends. I loved my cubby where I kept my Star Wars–themed Darth Vader sneakers. And I especially loved my teacher, Mrs. Hubert, who described me in report cards as a cooperative child excelling in all areas, writing, "Phil contributes to group discussions and has a good background of general knowledge. He is a well-liked child and an industrious pupil."

———

I arrived in first grade, just down the hall, where instead of colorful mats we sat at upright desks. Instead of story time, I was handed pencils and notebooks and told to copy letters off the board. My new classmates started writing. They mastered one letter after another. They wrote each letter perfectly within the lines of their composition notebooks. They named each letter and made the sound associated with it. They combined these letters to form words. I sat and I watched. I looked at the letters and tried to copy them. But I also realized something was very wrong. The letters didn't look right. I drew shapes, but they never formed into letters.

On Monday mornings, my teacher gave me a list of spelling words. I was expected to memorize them by Friday. On Fridays when I took the test, a searing pain hit my stomach because I knew I would fail. When it was over, I handed my test to the person behind me to be graded. I prayed Trudy Nickerson could keep a secret.

One day my classroom was divided into two groups. Each one was based on spelling ability: the A word group and the B word group. By the fourth week of school and my third zero on a test, the teacher announced to the class, "For the first time in all my years of teaching, I'm establishing a third reading group because Philip can't keep up."

———————

My teacher didn't want to pass me on to the next grade, but my mom pleaded my case. In second grade, my subjects expanded and so did my daily routine of copying down notes from the board. The other children looked up at what Mrs. Roy wrote, taking in a few words at a time like swimmers coming up for breath between strokes. I drew each letter one at a time. Before I could finish a single word, Mrs. Roy started cleaning the board. I started to count how many years I had left of school. My seven-year-old mind found the figure overwhelming.

———————

By third grade, the children were ready to read chapter books. Mrs. Douglas had the class read *Charlotte's Web* aloud, each child reading one paragraph at a time. I counted the number of students ahead of me and tried to find which passage would torture me. I tried to read with the intense focus of someone defusing a bomb. Mrs. Douglas let me struggle with the first word.

"Wa . . ." I said. Then I tried again. "Wa-ha . . ." And again. "Wa-ha-ree."

"Where's," Mrs. Douglas said. "The word is 'where's.'"

Next word.

"Pa . . . Puh . . . Puh-puh . . . Pay . . ."

"Papa," she said.

"*Paw*-puh," I repeated.

Two down.

"G—" I started.

"Where's Papa going with that ax?" she interjected. She told the student behind me to read on. I realized my heart was racing. I was sweating. Shaking. It took several more pages of story to realize that Papa was about to kill Wilbur with the ax.

Mrs. Douglas assigned a test about Canada's provinces and territories. She gave me a zero out of twelve. But not every answer was wrong. My right answers, she said, were spelled wrong. Mrs. Douglas took issue with my spelling, my coloring, my scissor skills. She said I lacked commitment to the square-dancing unit. I wore my cousin's old AC/DC T-shirts that went down to my knees. "You need to come to class in clothes that fit you," she told me. I thought, lady, this shirt is the least of my problems.

One day in December I got another zero on a math sheet, and she sent it home with me for my parents to sign. I gave it to my mom, and she said, "Philip, why did you leave this blank?"

"I didn't," I said. "I just filled out the back by accident."

She turned the worksheet over. "But on this side, the ink just bled through. All the numbers are backwards. You couldn't tell, dear?"

"No."

"Hmm. You actually got most of them right."

"Mrs. Douglas is pretty mad."

"Well, I'm impressed, Delphi," she said and signed it. She called me Philip when I was in trouble, Delphi when she wanted to double down on support.

As the Fs from Mrs. Douglas kept rolling in, my evening home-work ritual intensified. After school, my mom allowed me to decompress until dinner. Then we spent hours at the big oak table in the kitchen. Once a week I was driven forty-five minutes up the highway to a tutor. Nothing seemed to help. No one knew why I couldn't read. My mom also started volunteering at the school. She appeared to simply assist the librarian, Mrs. Sinova, but it was really a covert operation to ensure I was receiving fair treatment.

Toward the end of the year, I visited Toronto, where a learning disability specialist referred me to the children's hospital. Doctors examined my eyes. They scanned my brain. They stuck thirty-two needles into my head. Still no answers. At night, I prayed. Every night I prayed. I prayed that I'd wake up smart.

———

Mrs. Slate told the class to read twenty pages from our textbooks, then put our heads on our desks when finished. It was fourth grade, and reading felt like threading a needle with an impossibly small hole. During those reading sessions, I started to develop a talent for performative comprehension. I picked out a midlevel reader in class and turned the page when they did, knitted my brow and smirked to myself as if I'd read something funny, then nodded my head like, "Wow, this author really gets me."

Looking at a block of text was like trying to memorize an abstract painting. I developed an up-close and personal relationship with each letter. Ds I loved. They were honest and sincere. Ds always sounded like Ds. Fs were cool. Ls were harmless. But all other twenty-three letters were not to be trusted. *H* could double-cross you. The eighth letter in the alphabet was like the eight ball in billiards. Use it the wrong way and it's game over. Look no further than my name: Phil Hanley. First *H* has the audacity to conspire with *P* to put *F* out of a job. A split second later, it's back to looking out for itself.

I was convinced that without the letter *H*, most troubling words would cease to exist. There would be no mistaking *throw* for *through*. There would be no *thought, though, thorough, there, they're, their, hair, heir, hour, our. Rhyme* or *rhythm.*

In class I panted out *H* sounds. Just get this fucking thing out of me, I thought to myself. *H* convinced me the game was rigged. My teachers were blackjack dealers and the house always won.

———

Mrs. Simmons was an academic resource teacher. She had resting teacher voice and her hair was a shade of burgundy normally reserved for rental cars. I spent every English period working with her on reading exercises that weren't very helpful but at least spared me the embarrassment of struggling in front of my peers. We met in her office, a converted janitor's closet that smelled of ammonia. One day in May, she brought me into the office, but I didn't see the usual books or worksheets. She spoke to me: "Starting in September, you'll be attending Ritson Road. You'll be placed in a special class. It's an aid class where you'll be given more individual attention."

"Special ed?" I said, and I began to cry.

"You're actually very lucky," she said. "There are limited spots."

"You're saying it's hard to get into special ed?"

She started going over the details, but I was in another world. I didn't know anyone at Ritson Road. No more running around the playground with Liam singing "Jumpin' Jack Flash." No more walking to lunch at Danny Birch's house to eat fruit roll-ups and play with his cat.

She sent me back to Mrs. Slate's class but I took a detour to the bathroom. I wet a wad of paper towel and pressed it to my eyes, inhaling its sawdust scent. I blew my nose until the paper made it sting. I pulled it together before going back to class. The second I got home I fell apart.

"I promise you it won't be as bad as you think it is," my mom said. "And you can have Liam and Danny over after school any time you want."

"By the time we get home it's almost dark out. They won't be allowed!" I ran to my room and slammed the door.

The following September I stood outside my house on a gray morning at 7:00 a.m. waiting for the short bus to arrive. The first day my mom had driven me, and it had taken a brisk fifteen minutes. But some days she needed to work. I chose an empty seat in the middle but crouched down in the aisle, not wanting anyone in the neighborhood to catch sight of me through the window. When I exited, I tried to hide in the middle of the pack, but the short bus was half the size of a regular bus and had the same number of lights and signs. It was as inconspicuous as a winning slot machine.

The special ed class was in a small, drafty room near the far exit of the building. There were six of us and two teachers—Mr. Chandler and Mrs. Bryer. Mr. Chandler sat on his desk pontificating at us for hours. He had a habit of violently scratching his scalp and then inspecting his nails. I spent most of the fall and winter learning Christmas carols for the school holiday concert. The following semester I turned my attention to weaving, painstakingly constructing my own looms before spending weeks making a single place mat. I was so miserable I started to miss the days when the only thing different about me was being unable to read.

I didn't know why but I returned to my old school, S.J. Phillips, for sixth grade. At first I thought the year of weaving had cured me and my special ed days were behind me. But then I learned my parents had pulled me from Ritson Road. I hadn't made progress. It turned out that learning medieval textile techniques did not benefit kids with learning disabilities. I was back at S.J. Phillips, but my return was bittersweet. I was even further behind my classmates than before. I couldn't even copy off them.

I failed everything. I even failed math, something I had always been good at, because I couldn't read the word problems. I got the calculations right but lost marks for misspelling or miswording the conclusions. During a parent-teacher conference, my homeroom teacher told my mom she had no choice but to fail me. My mom explained that my problem was with writing and reading, not math. My teacher said if she made an exception for me, she'd have to make an exception for everyone.

My parents paid for more testing in Toronto. The doctors finally diagnosed me. I had severe dyslexia, a learning difference that essentially means I process language differently than others do. It had been five years of struggling. Of not knowing what was wrong with me. Of trying and failing and weaving, so much weaving. But now there was a word. It's who I am. It's what will define me for the rest of my life. And I'll never even be able to spell it.

———————

The next year I attended junior high at Central Park Senior Public School. On the first day, all three hundred students went to the gym and sat on the hardwood floor while teachers called out their students' names. I pieced together that a young, handsome guy with his sleeves rolled up was Mr. Raymond, my special ed teacher. I had been dreading this moment all summer—him calling my name in front of the whole school, outing me, separating me from the rest. But he called only seven names—all boys—and they filed out of the gym without me. Before long all the classes had left and it was just me and another boy, Steve Love, sitting on an empty basketball court.

Steve looked annoyed and I adopted the same expression, like "Get it together, guys," though secretly I was elated. I sat until the vice principal came over, took our names, and directed us to Mr. Raymond's class. I would be marooned here for the next two years.

But it wasn't all bad. Junior high had band, and all summer I had looked forward to joining, hoping to play drums. With Mr. Raymond's permission, I left special ed and walked to the basement, where the music room was located, to attend the first class. Kids were already there, goofing around, using the brass instruments to make fart sounds and using water spray for the trumpet valves like breath mist. The vibe was noisy and fun. I sat right up front and the teacher came in and took attendance. When my name wasn't on the list, she asked, "Oh, is this your homeroom? Has this been happening to you all day?"

"No, I came from Mr. Raymond's class," I said.

"I see. Hmm. Well, band isn't offered to students in his class."

I decided to try art.

Mrs. Occer noticed that I had customized my whole outfit. My T-shirt was covered with paint splatter and I had drawn checkers on my yellow Chuck Taylors. I finally made a good first impression. One of my projects was to draw a realistic portrait. "Flesh tones only, please," she told the class. "Except Phil, who can use any color he wants."

I also got to leave Mr. Raymond's class for math, science, and French. I excelled at math. Numbers made sense to me. Science and French were disastrous. Being put in French seemed particularly optimistic. "He can't read or write in English . . . let's give French a whirl."

But the rest of my time was spent in Mr. Raymond's class, eight of us, with varying degrees of disability. Shane Foot was eleven, nearly six feet tall, with the kind of barrel chest that implied he could hold his own in a barroom brawl, if ever an eleven-year-old found himself in such a situation. His mom worked nights and let him and his older brother run wild. We bonded over our love of heavy metal music, but it turned out that's all we had in common. He seemed to have the same scope of sexual knowledge as Dr. Ruth and cornered me in the bathroom to try to force-feed me hash and tell me graphic sex stories that even now, as an adult, I would have trouble topping.

Jeremy also followed me around. He was funny, hyper, and nowadays would be diagnosed with ADHD. He would be up and joking around or in high spirits and Mr. Raymond would force him to sit still at his desk for hours. It was torture for him. Sometimes, he'd lower his head into his hands and cry.

Will was the only kid who seemed happy to be there. He raised his hand in class and actually bothered to write down assignments with the intention of completing them. He fell just as short as the rest of the group academically but had a "we'll get 'em next time" attitude that I found objectionable. The game was rigged against him. He hadn't figured out he'd already lost.

And we weren't even the worst students in school.

Next door, Mr. Campbell taught students with even greater needs. Our classes were often combined for lessons, and we took our bathroom breaks together between periods. While other students walked in cliques down the halls, yelling and laughing at their lockers, we were shuttled through the crowds like oversize toddlers.

We took day trips to places like the GM factory and two nuclear plants. "Being equidistant from two nuclear sites," the guide told us, "Oshawa is an ideal target for a terrorist attack." At least we have that going for us, I thought.

The next spring, the school held a flag football tournament over the course of a few lunch periods. My special ed class competed against another eighth-grade class, which had some of the best athletes in the school. After I heard Ryan Ward, a star football player, say this would be like competing in the Special Olympics, I volunteered to be quarterback. The game was played on a soccer field behind the school, with only pylons marking the end zones. We strapped into our red flag football belts and huddled around Mr. Raymond. "Will, you go deep," he said. Will, decked out in a brand-new Toronto Argonauts jersey, nodded and said, "You got it, Coach!"

I rolled my eyes.

I approached the line of scrimmage where the blue team was lined up. Under my breath, I said to Jeremy, "I'm gonna hand it to you. Just run as fast as you can."

Shane Foot hiked the ball then protected the pocket like a roadie guarding the backstage at a rock concert. The blue team, like Mr. Raymond, expected us to throw, so their coverage was deep as I shoved the ball into Jeremy's hands and he took off down the field with his spastic energy and herky-jerky gait. By the time the other class realized that they had to approach this bucking bronco of a kid, he was almost all the way down the field. Finally, Ryan Ward caught up to him. Jeremy ducked to avoid one of Ryan's flailing hands, which managed to grab his flag just ten yards from the end zone.

"Got his freak flag," Ryan said, with more pride about his joke than anything else.

We huddled up again. Mr. Raymond congratulated me on moving the ball but was quick to add, "Let's call plays that are most likely to lead to success. Will, try to get open."

As I approached the line, I repeated Mr. Raymond's instructions loud enough for the other team to hear. Ryan Ward spread the word. "Look for Special Will in the end zone!"

Shane hiked the ball to me and again I handed it to Jeremy, who was standing beside me out of habit. But as soon as the ball touched his hands, he took off again, this time with a clear path straight past the pylons. He scored. Jeremy ran toward me with a look of disbelief and we embraced in a sweaty hug. Shane taunted the blue team by graphically humping the air. With his intimidation tactics and my offbeat chemistry with Jeremy, we won the game. In the two years we passed through Central Park, not one of us would make a single sports team. But that day we returned as winners to the class that everyone associated with losers.

———

High school. Finally, high school. I saw the light at the end of the tunnel.

Inside the Learning Resource Center, Mrs. Tailor led class in a windowless room made entirely out of painted cinder blocks, the white walls and fluorescent lighting giving it a menacing brightness. There were posters everywhere. Big ones with black backgrounds, single-serif words, inspirational quotations, photos of sunsets and rock climbers. Next to the chalkboard was a poster with a kitten hanging from a branch and the words "Hang in There!" I was almost out. It was almost done.

Mrs. Tailor was obsessed with Maslow's hierarchy of needs and had a poster for that too. In one of our first lessons, she asked me to read out loud from the base of the hierarchy pyramid.

I took a stab at it.

"Psychological needs."

"Nope. Here's a hint. Air, water, shelter . . . think of your body."

"Physical needs?"

"Close," she says. "Physiological. Try the next one."

"Yeah, I'm out," I said. "I can't read."

"Can't isn't a word we use in this classroom," she responded.

"I *cannot* read," I said.

I had to endure the toxic positivity of her resource class for the next three years, but because most of my classes were outside of it, I could move through the halls with some ease, like a normal student, a normal kid. My locker was on the first floor of the building, a mess of crumpled-up assignments, loose paper, and unused binders, all crushed under the weight of my skateboard. The locker next to mine belonged to a kid everyone called Pugs. He wore khakis and sweaters and looked like he was about to shake your hand and thank you for your vote.

Pugs was close with my friend Tommy Love, but we hadn't hung out much. I was a freshman and they were sophomores. Lately I'd started to realize that none of my friends were in my grade. I was so far removed from my actual classmates that they might as well have been in a different school. But Tommy and his friends in the sophomore class embraced me. Even though Pugs was only a year older than me, he had what my fourteen-year-old self considered a superpower: he had gone gray prematurely and looked old enough to buy alcohol. We pooled our allowances together. We walked to the liquor store, where Pugs went in and selected a magnum of almost undrinkable red wine, and before attempting to purchase it, just to squelch any suspicion, he asked the clerk questions like "Does this pair well with lamb chops?"

Pugs was the only son of strict Scottish immigrants. Their house was pristine, and Pugs's room had clearly been decorated by his mother. He slept in one of two twin beds, always perfectly made. There was a framed picture of a butterfly and lots of crocheted knickknacks. He worked at the fish department in Miracle Mart so he always had plenty of spending money. He bought himself the first computer I had ever seen: a Commodore 64. He was the most loved out of all my friends and also the most fucked with.

One night some friends and I snuck into his garage in the middle of the night, started his lawnmower, and then phoned his house. I told whoever answered the phone to "Turn off your fucking mower!" One year, over winter break, in the middle of the night, we dismantled the elaborate Christmas decorations from Pugs's neighbor's house across the street, and put them up on Pugs's house instead.

Pugs and I made an unlikely duo. Pugs was always on time; I was chronically late. He ironed his shirts; I sometimes showed up to class in pajamas. He was at the top of his class; I got mostly Ds. But he never looked down on me. He was kind and confident in who he was.

Pugs took me to my first high school party, at the house of a girl named Tracy. Tracy was in tenth grade and lived a few blocks from Central Park School. Her parents were gone for the weekend, and when my dad dropped us off, we walked to her backyard where a bunch of people sat on coolers and lawn chairs or stood around drinking. I spotted my friend Tommy. He led me inside to the washroom, then took out and unfolded a piece of cigarette foil to reveal a tiny red pill.

"It's so small," I said.

"Small? This is a double-barrel strawberry. It's twice the size of a California sunshine," he said. Tommy had purchased the five-dollar acid at Leisure Amusements, an arcade downtown. I had started drinking and smoking weed, and this seemed like the logical next step. I placed it under my tongue.

Back in the party, I began to feel nauseated but for some reason couldn't stop smiling. An hour passed. I looked down and my hand was iridescent. I walked back into the house and made my way downstairs to a back room in the basement. There was a texturized linoleum floor and a single pull-chain bulb I yanked and turned on. The light bounced off the shiny floor and illuminated every peak and valley, revealing its majestic pattern to me. How had I not seen it before!

I leaned against the storage freezer. Pugs walked in. As he got closer, I could tell he'd been smoking weed.

"What are you doing in here?" he asked.

"Chillin'," I said, my eyes trained to the vinyl.

"Do I look weird?" he asked. I turned to look him in the face. He looked normal to me, maybe a little pale, but before I could tell him this, his face started sinking in on itself.

"What's wrong?" he asked. "Why are you staring at me?" He brought his hands to his face. "Are you high? Am I high?"

———

My mom understood. She was an avid reader and had never had more than one drink in a sitting. Yet she got me. She looked the other way when I put off chores or slept until noon. If I came home smelling like weed, she accepted my explanation that a friend of mine had been smoking American cigarettes. When I turned sixteen, she let me share her car, a blue Volkswagen Jetta that I covered in Grateful Dead stickers. When she drove on the highway, white dudes with dreadlocks honked at her and flashed peace signs.

My mom understood. But she was far from a pushover. She had strength. Joan was the eldest of eight girls. All their names started with the letter J. Which is no easy task. Her household was hectic, and she was expected to pick up the parenting slack. I'd seen a photo of my mom at age nine that reminded me of the ones you see of children working in coal mines. Instead of being covered in soot, she's covered in Js—Joyce, June, and Josephine.

My mom's Ken Burns–worthy upbringing didn't make her hard. Instead, she showed mercy. While she was pregnant with me, she had worked teaching children with disabilities. Then I came along, and she also did it at home. When it was time to do homework, she came to the kitchen table armed with enough positivity for the two of us.

"I'm just dumb," I said. "We all know it. Why do I have to take a science test to prove it?"

"No no no, dear. Of course you're not," she said. "Look, you got the last two questions on the practice quiz right!"

"Yeah, after I got the first eight wrong," I said.

She put her arm around me. She looked me in the eye. "You're not dumb," she said. "Don't let anyone tell you that."

———

Oshawa wasn't called the Dirty Shwa for nothing. It was the '90s but my town felt as though it was living in a 1980s metal music video. Every Friday after school I was on the phone trying to buy oil, hash, weed, acid, mushrooms, and, when I could find it, mescaline. I took acid on Friday night and went home on Saturday then was back with my friends later that night, where I had to double the dosage just to feel the effect. By Sunday I was a total wreck and could barely cope with the thought of returning to school. I lived for basement reprieves with my friends. Among them was Shalom. Shalom was tall, thin, a hippie, danced ballet, the type of girl people said could be a model. She floated around groups, sometimes joining my friends for drug-filled nights, sometimes off doing her own thing.

Shalom's house was between my school and my house, so some days I walked her home. Her mom always greeted me with a smile and was one of the only parents who didn't judge me for having long hair. She complimented me on my appearance and said I had charisma. One time while greeting her, my dyslexia kicked in. Instead of calling her Sandy, I called her Nancy. For the rest of high school, in my company she called herself Nancy.

My mornings were spent in Mrs. Tailor's Special Needs Bunker, and I wasn't alone. There were six of us in the class, hormonal teenage boys with hormonal teenage frustrations. The kid next to me, David Ash, struggled with reading as much as I did but handled it differently. When Mrs. Tailor left the room, he flipped over the desks. When she returned, we all denied knowing who did it. Kenny Rudd was incensed that he couldn't wear his mirrored sunglasses in class even though they were prescription.

Mrs. Tailor's class functioned as special ed, homeroom, English, and a supervised free period. During English she read young adult adventure books out loud to us. While Pugs dove into *Beowulf* and *Heart of Darkness*, I sunk my teeth into *Crab!*, a coming-of-age story set in Manitoba. Even though I tested above average for math, they put me in the remedial class, which was taught by the gym teacher. I failed two years in a row. Science I also failed two years in a row—three including summer school.

In middle school I had at least been somewhat engaged by school, but by eleventh grade I'd checked the hell out. The only real calculation that interested me was the maximum number of truancies I could receive without being expelled. I was late sixty-eight times in a single semester.

When I did make it to class, I got up to sharpen my pencil as much as possible. I walked to the wall-mounted sharpener, emptied it out regardless of whether there were any shavings, then returned to my desk to try to relieve myself from the excruciating boredom with a number of methods I called "Philing time." I counted how long it took to dissolve a Tic Tac in my mouth. I colored large portions of paper with pencil, then created images in the darkness with my eraser.

But soon I gave up trying to distract myself. I was so bored. I sat and stewed. I was accused of daydreaming, but my thoughts weren't anywhere else. They were as stuck at my desk as I was, day after day, where I was reminded how stupid I was. The school bell rang. The classes emptied. The reminders stayed with me. I was stupid and there was no escaping it.

One night I picked up a friend in north Oshawa and aimlessly drove along the outskirts of the city. The roads were icy, and as we approached a red light, I braked too late, rear-ended the car in front of us, and badly crashed the Volkswagen. I should have felt relieved that I wasn't injured. Instead, I was disappointed because I was unharmed and had to return to school.

My parents asked me to go see a therapist. My mom took me to a guy in Toronto who specialized in "troubled youth." As soon as I sat down, he said, "Just so you know, if you tell me anything about drugs, sex, or dangerous behavior, I'll be obligated to tell your parents." So I said nothing.

Mrs. Tailor suggested my parents purchase a Dictaphone. The idea was simple. I was to record my teachers' lessons so I could listen to them later while studying. But most lessons were written on the blackboard. After the first day I realized it wouldn't work. While on one of my bi-hourly bathroom visits, I got an idea. I made a quick recording, then headed back to marketing class. Mr. White was midsentence when I hit Play and the sound of a flushing toilet interrupted him.

"Give me that!" he said.

"Give me that!" the Dictaphone echoed.

———

After the car accident, my parents wouldn't let me drive a car, so I bought a cherry-red Yamaha scooter, but soon the Canadian winter set in and I had no other form of transportation. I was late so often that my mornings usually started with a trip to the principal's office. I'd roll in twenty minutes late and be greeted by Ms. Harper, the school secretary, who'd take pity on me and waive the mandatory detention.

One day while I was walking Shalom home, she told me about the Cure concert she'd just gone to in Toronto. "Someone actually gave me a business card and said to call him," she told me. "He's from a modeling agency."

"That's cool," I said. "Everyone has always said you could do that. You gonna do it?"

"Maybe," she said. "They want me to do some test shoots back in Toronto. It'll probably be nothing. But Phil? Don't tell anyone. Okay?"

"Sure thing," I said.

Shalom drove to Toronto. She did the test shoots. She came home, but soon she was gone again and never returned. She became a model. She shot with Flea from the Red Hot Chili Peppers. She appeared in *Vogue*. She was sixteen years old, and her life was starting. I was excited for her to get out of Oshawa. We kept in touch. But behind my excitement lay envy. I was still home, still smoking weed and listening to the Grateful Dead with Pugs and Tommy, and still a kid in school who couldn't read.

Before the school year ended, I had a meeting with my guidance counselor, Mr. Cynar, to discuss future plans. When I walked into his office, he looked me up and down, smirked, and said, "I guess this is what they call grunge." Despite my dismal grades, I held on to the hope that a college education might still be possible. I expected Mr. Cynar to lay out my options and give me a strongly worded warning to buckle down in class. Instead, he looked at my transcript and said, "Well, college is not really an option considering you've taken only remedial courses."

"I was forced to take those subjects," I said. "I wanted to take some advanced classes, but they said I couldn't because special ed students aren't allowed."

"Well, in any case, college is a low probability. What do you plan to do instead?"

I had no answer to that one. "What do you think I should do?" I asked.

"I'm an academic adviser," he said. "Anything else is out of my wheelhouse."

I left fuming. I was so mad I skipped the rest of the school day. Mr. Cynar was no different from every teacher I'd ever had. He was just less subtle in telling me what everyone else already knew but refused to say: I was a lost cause. Had my grades been great? No. Had I showed up to the meeting high? Yes. But it wouldn't have mattered either way. They took one look at me and my file and decided I was doomed to a life of name tags and coworkers with neck tattoos. When my parents got home, I unloaded on them.

"That peckerhead," my dad said. "You can take whatever you goddamn want. My taxes pay his salary."

My mom and dad scheduled a meeting with my latest special ed teacher, Mr. Armstrong, to discuss my fate. He explained to them why he also believed I was ill-equipped to take advanced courses. My parents were not satisfied. Finally, it was decided that I would be allowed to change my schedule if they signed a letter acknowledging that the school's educators advised against it. Once an agreement was reached, my mom marched into the school and insisted that she and Mr. Armstrong sit down a second time to go through the results of all my testing since my diagnosis.

In September, Pugs and Tommy both went to Queen's University, two and a half hours away. With my friends gone and little to distract me, I began my final year of high school. With the arrangement negotiated between my parents and the school, I signed up for advanced classes. The first day I walked in, I was greeted like a new kid. Everyone else was deep into the university application process, and all they wanted to talk about was campus visits and test scores and early admission. There was a sense of optimism in the air that I had never experienced.

For each of my four advanced classes, I had a one-on-one resource period with Mr. Armstrong. We worked at a round table in the middle of his classroom, our chairs pushed next to each other. We went over the material from my last class then worked through as much homework as we could before our time together ran out. Mr. Armstrong had notified all my teachers that I needed to be provided with class notes, but I almost always had to bring it up myself. If a test was coming up, I'd walk to the teacher's desk and quietly remind them, then they'd choose someone, always a girl, always with good handwriting, and very publicly announce, "Marcy, Phil needs to borrow your notes please." I'd walk to the student, collect her notes apologetically, and promise to bring them to her next class right after I made photocopies.

For winter exams, the other students were given ninety minutes to complete each exam, while Mr. Armstrong and I had as much time as I needed. I took all day. He read me each question, then I dictated my answers. For geography, I might be asked to name the seven layers of rock: metamorphic, sedimentary, igneous, and so on. For the normal test, I would have had to memorize each layer and how to spell it. For my test, Mr. Armstrong would read the questions, then I'd examine the test and ask him to repeat himself until the sounds in my head matched the questions on the page. Then I'd dictate the names of rocks while he spelled them out. It was intense and exhausting work.

Mr. Armstrong was serious, punctual, and favored a particular sweater vest because, as he told me, his wife said he looked good in red. During the exams I was not allowed to leave his classroom, except for escorted trips to the bathroom. He stayed in the classroom too, and we ate our packed lunches together: sandwiches in paper bags, leftovers in Tupperware. I recharged my batteries by trying to get him to talk shit about the other teachers. He never told. But one time I questioned the dedication of one of his colleagues. In between bites, his expression changed, and he simply said, "That's very astute."

The exam results came back, and I couldn't believe the news. I got all As. Reading and writing hadn't gotten easier, but I'd worked harder than ever, and with my parents' support and Mr. Armstrong's help, it had all paid off. I was determined to keep it up. I cut out drinking and drugs and turned down invitations to concerts and weekends away. After class I sat at the kitchen table with my mom, completing unfinished homework. I became aware of the grade scale for the first time and was hell-bent on letting no assignments slip by. The end of the school year approached and I did nothing but agonize over my grades. I worked myself to exhaustion.

Near the end of May, I woke up with a throat swollen up so badly I struggled to breathe, and I went to the emergency room. I had mono. I missed two weeks of school. All my life I'd wanted an excuse to miss school, and now when I was finally motivated, I was derailed against my will. I begged my mom to let me go back. "You've finished most of your major assignments," she told me. "You'll be okay. You are okay."

I recovered just in time for graduation. I walked across the stage as an honors student. I was named an Ontario Scholar and the Most Improved Student, and I received an award named for a beloved law teacher who'd recently passed away. Mr. Armstrong wrote me a note in which he apologized for discouraging me from taking advanced classes. "Your desire was translated into overwhelming effort," he wrote. "You were the architect of your success."

I talked to my parents about going to college. I'd just graduated from high school, against all odds, and assumed this was the next step. When they avoided giving me a straight answer, I knew something was up. One night they called me to the back porch. I sat outside, on the wooden deck, in front of the in-ground pool.

"Listen, Phil," my father said. "You know we're proud of you."

"I know," I said. I thought of the years my mom sat with me. I thought of how they fought for me. I leaned in toward him.

"But you know, college is a big thing. You proved you could get through high school. But . . ." He paused. "But look at what it took. Look at the toll it took on you. You can't risk pushing yourself so hard."

I sat back. I understood. I was relieved now to know the truth. The goal was to qualify, never to actually do it. That was victory enough. The reality was so clear that my father didn't have to elaborate. It was so clear that everyone knew it but never had to say it. And now that I was here, on the back porch listening to the bugs buzzing in the Oshawa night, I accepted that my education was complete.

What do you do when you're eighteen years old and out of school and have no plans for the future? What do you do when you can't read without the support of a parent or teacher? What job do you apply for, what career is out there for you to pursue? How do you glide through the days, weeks, and months living at home, circling through Oshawa like a mouse unable to find his way out of a maze? What do you do when your friend Shalom calls out of the blue and asks, Are you still tall? and Are you still lean? and Have you ever thought of doing male modeling? and you know that there is only one right answer.

2

Poser

The Giusti Residence, with sliding metal shades covering the windows, resembled an army barracks more than a hotel. I paid the driver who'd taken me here from the airport. He'd spoken nonstop Italian the whole way, as if I'd pick it up the more he spoke. With most of the cash I'd brought with me now in his hand, he zipped away, I assumed still talking. But I was in Milan, on the eve of fashion season.

The inside of the Giusti wasn't much more welcoming than the combat-ready exterior. The barren walls and linoleum floors reminded me of my elementary school, which felt like a bad omen. An unshaven man with a cigarette that should have been ashed a while ago stood behind the worn front desk. I gave him my name and he consulted a giant notebook. Muttering in Italian, he handed me a key that looked like it could unlock a pirate chest. "Six floor," he grunted without looking up.

"Where's the elevator?" I asked.

He smiled through an exhalation of smoke and pointed at the stairwell.

Panting and sweating, I unlocked the door to my shoebox-size room. The space was spartan: a pair of twin beds that kind of folded up into couches, a window darkened by the metal shades I had seen from the street, a small kitchenette, and a small white plastic table like those often found on patios in the New World. It seemed inhumane to expect a person to live in such a claustrophobic space.

I collapsed onto the hard mattress, exhausted from the red-eye. Finally, sleep. What seemed like moments later, I woke up, panicked at the sound of the door creaking open. Trying to assess if this was a dream, I sprang to my feet. My eyes struggled to adjust to the dark as a bulky shadow moved toward me.

"Morning, roomie, I'm Andrew," the figure said. He dropped his bag and took off his T-shirt the way most people would kick off their shoes, as if to say, "Where are my manners?" It was like he was raised by models. Andrew was excessively muscular, built like a classical sculpture if Michelangelo had used frat boys as his muse. Shirtless, Andrew actually looked like he should be in Milan—I bet when he told people he was a model they weren't surprised. When I'd informed my best friend Pugs I was going to give it a whirl, he'd replied, "Just your face, right?"

"Phil," I mumbled, loathing this development of a roommate.

Andrew pulled a can of tuna out of his carry-on, peeled back the lid, and offered me some.

"No thanks," I said.

"Oh, you already had breakfast?"

Andrew rummaged around the small drawer beside the stovetop

burner and retrieved our one fork. "This place is too small for me to do my squat walks," he informed me through a mouthful of tuna.

"Your what?"

"What do you do for your legs?" he asked.

"Nothing. I guess I've been taking them for granted all these years."

Truth was, I kept my legs concealed at all times. They were remarkably skinny, and my knees were oddly pronounced, like they belonged to a prehistoric bird of prey. I hadn't worn shorts in public since I was a kid.

"Most guys train their legs once, maybe twice a week," Andrew continued. "Me? Two-four-seven. My place back home is a two-bedroom one-and-a-half bath and I squat walk everywhere." Andrew demonstrated, dropping down and walking like a chimpanzee from one side of the room to the other. I had never related to a human less.

"I deliberately leave things in different rooms, so I have to squat walk to get them," he continued, crisscrossing our micro room.

"Like in the half bath?" I asked.

Andrew nodded as if to say "exactly." "Try it," he instructed midway through lap five.

"I'd rather die," I said, expecting some reaction. But Andrew remained unfazed.

Andrew popped the last piece of dry tuna in his mouth and sat cross-legged on his bed. "I'm from Phoenix," he said, taking out his book: a portfolio filled with modeling photos. As I would soon learn, male models in Milan carried their books everywhere. They were proof that as grown men we played dress-up for a living and hoped to get to do it more.

"Go for it," Andrew said, handing me his book. I immediately regretted not saving my "I'd rather die" line.

Andrew's portfolio didn't contain much modeling work. It was almost all test shoots. I tried not to smirk at a black-and-white photo of Andrew in a desert landscape, pulling up a pair of tight pants. I wondered what peculiar series of events would lead to a man having to hastily put on a pair of pleather pants in the desert. The next photo showed him in a child's inflatable pool, splashing around in a pair of white briefs. His muscles bulged and glistened. This shoot raised even more questions.

"Before I became a model, I was going to school to be an anesthesiologist, assisting Dr. Constantine Peters," Andrew said, as I leafed through his book. "He's probably the most famous anesthesiologist in the greater Phoenix area. I was his protégé."

"He's the best in the business," I said.

"That gig, you're basically playing God. People can die on the table. I had people's lives in my hands every day."

I examined a photo of Andrew with grease smeared on his face and chest, seductively leaning over the hood of a car, implying that he may have just made love to a Chevy Nova.

"You like that one?" he asked. "It's my favorite too."

"You gave up a medical career to do this?" I asked, handing him back his book, hoping I wouldn't see those images when I closed my eyes.

"Hell yeah. I was at a pool party, and an agent came up to me and said I could be the next big thing. People have *always* told me I should model, but this guy hooked it up. Within two weeks I booked this."

Andrew flipped open his book to reveal a shot of his feet in a pair of Birkenstocks. I thought there might be something more, but that was it. The setup looked amateur, taken in a strip mall photo studio.

"Sweet, an ad?" I asked.

"Campaign. For a shoe store in a massive mall just outside of Phoenix," Andrew said. "My agent called me and said, 'Don't ask any questions, just go get a pedicure.' That's how I booked it. It's the little things like that that get you ahead in this business."

I'll keep that in mind if I want my feet to be locally famous in the Southwest, I thought, but all I said was "thanks."

"Don't mention it. I'm just paying it forward." Andrew looked lovingly at the picture of his sandaled feet. "Lots of eyeballs saw my tootsies."

I desperately needed sleep, but Andrew launched into a lecture on making it as a model. "Diet and exercise are critical. It's a lifestyle."

"Cool. Well, I got to get some sleep."

"Yeah, you do," Andrew agreed, peering at my face. "But you know what would help the bags under your eyes more than sleep?"

I was on the edge of my bed, and not just because it was so fucking tiny.

"Preparation H," Andrew said, then paused to give my mind time to finish being blown. "It gets rid of swelling."

"And dignity," I quipped.

Again, no reaction. That was strong, I thought. Deserved something.

"And drink plenty of water," Andrew continued. "Guess what percentage of the human body is made up of water?"

Internally, I was begging for mercy. Please let it stop.

Andrew ran his eyes up and down my lanky frame. "And you should start doing some push-ups."

"I'll start tomorrow," I said. "I really need to crash."

I woke to the sound of Andrew's heavy breathing. He was banging out sit-ups, fully dressed in a tight white tank top tucked into jeans with motorcycle boots. He looked like a backup dancer in a Janet Jackson video. I would learn this was his casting uniform, an outfit that always inspired him to say, "It's go time." I was severely congested, my eyes crusted over from Milan's pollution.

"I wasn't sure if I should wake you," Andrew said. "All the Ricardo Guy boys are heading to the agency. We're meeting in the lobby in fifteen."

Fuck, I thought, as I stepped into our weird shower that was three feet deep and two feet long. I had to hurry. I didn't want to miss my opportunity to travel with readers when I went to the agency for the first time.

I followed the Giusti boys to the metro and we shuttled from our pseudo-dormitory to the Ricardo Guy Agency, cramming into Tino's office, where I became painfully aware that I was the only skinny guy with long hair, the only dude not sporting a clean-cut, tan, square-jawed look. One Giusti mate looked at my shoulder-length hair and said, "You have Dolce and Gabbana attitude," which, a moment later, I realized was an insult. Composite cards—what models have instead of résumés, which emphasize jawlines over qualifications—covered all four walls and surrounded Tino's round desk: modeling mission control. His assistant Simon sat on the edge of the desk in an Armani suit, speaking Italian on the phone and diligently taking notes.

Tino made his grand entrance from a side room with a tape measure around his neck and a deviant smile on his face. Tino had long flowing hair. He wore a white linen shirt untucked and *very* undone. He looked like a brunette Fabio. A rattled-looking all-American model followed him, tucking his shirt in as he joined our group. Tino dragged his hand over Simon's unflinching shoulder on his way to his chair. Simon stood rigid, the stoic Smithers to Tino's Mr. Burns. "His measurements were correct. But it never hurts to check," Tino declared.

The first time I'd met Tino, he'd nicknamed me Canadese. I knew it meant Canadian in Italian, but it still sounded emasculating, as if I were part Canuck, part daisy. Which was fitting—I felt like a flower compared to the solid oak trees that were my colleagues.

After taking his seat, Tino turned to us and crossed his legs in a way that put Sharon Stone to shame. "Ciao bellas, are you ready to book lots of shows and make Mommy Tino proud?"

I scanned to see what my colleagues were doing. Were we supposed to nod at Mommy Tino? The moment passed, and Tino instructed Simon to hand out the call sheets with the addresses of our castings, called go-sees. All over Milan, dozens of complexes just like the Giusti brimmed with aspiring models. Over the next two weeks, thousands of us would descend upon go-sees, where our bodies would be eyeballed by the biggest designers in the world. Some would be chosen to walk runways. But typically, designers saw a thousand guys to fill twenty spots. Most of us would be rejected, sent packing.

As the models took the sheets one by one and headed out, Tino spotted me. "Canadese, come," he said, beckoning me with his well-manicured finger. "You're my . . . how do you say, Simon, like in poker?"

"Full house," Simon muttered.

Tino gave him a dirty look. "Not full house, stupido. You're my . . . wild card!"

I smiled politely, but wished he thought of me as his jackpot. Simon handed me my list of go-sees. I glanced down at them as I headed out. They might as well have been written in binary code. I couldn't even remotely make out the Italian addresses. I couldn't tell the name of the street from the Italian word for *street*. It filled me with anxiety akin to calling your partner the wrong name during sex. I had to deeply concentrate to decipher a single word, then somehow match it to an address, which I'd have to locate on a physical map. Then somehow figure out the closest metro station. It felt like a sadistic treasure hunt.

Suddenly Mommy Tino's gambling metaphor seemed fitting. I was relieved to see the Giusti crew still out in front of the agency. I was in the unique situation of considering them complete morons but also knowing their superior phonics skills were my lifeline.

Feeling like a hypocrite, I followed Andrew and the rest of the herd to my first go-see at Jean Paul Gaultier.

Gaultier had been dubbed the maestro of mayhem by the fashion press, because he dressed men in skirts and Madonna in the infamous cone bra. Gaultier was known for taking out ads seeking "Atypical models. The facially disfigured should not refrain from applying." Walking the runway in one of his famous sailor-boy get-ups could jumpstart a career. I thought me and my prepubescent physique might have a shot.

I followed the other models to the metro. The Americans immediately proceeded to use the handrails for a spirited pull-up competition, much to the horror of the Italian passengers. I hadn't had such an embarrassing commute since riding the short bus to my first day of special ed. I had an urge to take each Italian aside and say, "So sorry, I'm Canadian and couldn't do a pull-up if I wanted to."

Every model in town showed up to Gaultier's go-see, including a group of frightening-looking people who'd been scouted straight from the streets of Milan. In a dark hallway, Andrew and I found what we thought was the end of the long line. A gutter punk with cheetah spots dyed into his cropped hair and a pet rat shook his head, said something in Italian, and pointed his rodent down the stairwell.

We pushed past another four hundred models and took our place in a basement room. As the procession inched forward, a brawl broke out among the hopefuls. Apparently, someone had tried to cut in line. My first thought was maybe a black eye might give them the edge we were all looking for.

Four hours later I stood in front of Gaultier and handed over my book. Dressed in a blue-and-white cotton knit sweater and a long black kilt, he opened my book and asked, in his thick French accent, "Where are you from?"

"Canada."

"Ah, Canada," he said, quickly flipping through my book. Time seemed to stand still while I tried to force myself to name-drop our mutual friend Shalom. I almost retched trying to get it out. He closed my book and slid it over to his stylist, who appeared to be totally hairless apart from his long eyelashes. He opted out of opening it, instead sliding it back to me and saying, "Merci." I slunk out to the hot pollution outside, where Andrew joined me a few minutes later.

"First they both looked at my book. Then the gay Kojak asked me to take off my shirt," he said, beaming.

I was mystified that Andrew's brain had produced the nickname "gay Kojak." If Andrew ever said something remotely humorous, maybe someday I'd have pecs.

"Guess what fucking Jean Paul Gaultier said? 'Oh la la, that one's in the bag,'" Andrew said. "I'm one for one, baby."

———

I was used to seeing other people win. At age nineteen, I was a lanky, 115-pound Deadhead with shoulder-length hair who had never gone swimming publicly without a T-shirt on. In high school, we were given a multiple-choice aptitude test and told it would inform our futures. I implemented a technique I had developed years before wherein, rather than struggle to read the questions,

I would select answers based upon the eye-pleasing patterns they produced. When the results came in for the test I was delighted. Each student was asked to read their career options in front of the class. I got up and reported, "rodeo clown, tree surgeon, and rabbi." The class erupted. My teacher couldn't believe my chutzpah.

The summer after graduation, a typical day consisted of sleeping until 4:30 p.m. I would awaken to the sound of the garage door opening as my mom arrived home from work. I'd jump out of bed, run downstairs, and pretend to be in the middle of one of the chores she had listed on a notepad beside the phone. She'd ask, "How was your day?" and I'd sigh, implying, "No rest for the weary," as though it had taken nine hours to haul three items of recycling to the bin in the garage. I thought I was convincing enough to pull off these deceptions. But my mom was participating in this one-act play just to show me mercy. Like when she pretended to believe my girlfriend stayed over because she got separated from her friends, and I wasn't indulging my teenage hormones but was on a humanitarian mission. My dad would arrive home a couple of hours later and we'd eat dinner as a family. Then I'd grab my skateboard and head to the parking lot of my old orthodontist's office to perfect my kickflips.

My purgatory seemed to have no end in sight. All I knew was that my dad was in the insurance business and loathed it. I didn't want a job I hated. On top of this, he was a workaholic. His favorite expression when I was growing up was "Life's a bitch and then you die." Every time he proclaimed this, my mom would say, "Martin!" She took issue with the language, but I feel like a child psychologist would object to the sentiment. I felt like my dad was telling me, "Go out there and be the best Phil you can be and don't forget you got that big dirt nap coming up!"

When Pugs and all my friends left for college, I ate dinner every night with my parents while my contemporaries chugged vodka cokes out of flower vases, rode ironing boards down flights of stairs, and were charged with public indecency. They were thriving.

Worse yet, Shalom was also a world away. People in Oshawa bought *Vogue* to count the number of pages she appeared in, but to me Shalom was just a badass girl in my group of burnout friends. One Christmas she came back from Europe and, to celebrate a particularly lucrative job, bought a grapefruit-size ball of hash and smoked us all into oblivion. Since then she'd moved to New York.

At the end of the summer, when my parents and I were invited to a wedding in Connecticut, Shalom suggested I come visit her in New York. My parents dropped me off at her Ninth Street address, and as their car pulled away, I anxiously hit the buzzer. I could see her through the glass door, running down a grand spiral staircase. She opened the door, screamed, and wrapped her arms and legs around me like a koala. "I love that you're here!" she said.

Shalom's apartment was a giant prewar two-bedroom that smacked of teenage millionaire. The crown molding was painted gold, the walls a screaming yellow. I stepped over suitcases that appeared to have been detonated and piles of dangerous-looking stilettos. "Fuck, I meant to have someone clean!" she said as she lit a Du Maurier cigarette.

"Just one person?" I asked.

We headed out into the city. I was totally, uncontrollably enamored. Not with the supermodel on my arm but with the filthy, crowded, putrid streets of the East Village. It felt dangerous and not in an Oshawa way, where you could be diagnosed with a staring problem and punched in the face at any moment. It was a dangerous excitement, as if anything could happen at any moment. Every person we passed seemed to be aware of something I had only suspected about life. I found myself moved by the urban expanse in the same way others must feel gazing at the Grand Canyon. I was in the throes of a full-on spiritual experience.

Shalom chose an Indian place on Sixth Street and First Avenue. She clapped her hands with anticipation: this would be my first time trying Indian food. Sitting across from me, wolfing down dal, she caught me up on her life. Earlier that morning she'd flown in from Paris on Karl Lagerfeld's private jet. She'd been working constantly for the last three years, zigzagging from one hemisphere to another.

"So what the hell are you doing?" she asked.

"Eating . . . nom bread?"

"It's naan. With an *N*."

"Oh, they changed it?"

She didn't laugh. "I meant Oshawa. You're still there and you're suddenly cool with that?"

"I'm not cool with it but . . ." I started racking my brain for anything I'd achieved recently besides landing a flawless kickflip.

"You should model."

I thought I'd misheard. But she continued.

"I'm serious. How tall are you, six two? You have interesting bone structure. I mean, you look like a white Snoop Dogg." I was strangely flattered. She went on.

"I've got a shoot in Toronto next month. You should come. You'll meet the photographer, I'll bet they'll want to do some test shots . . . I mean I shoot with less attractive versions of you four times a week." I liked where this was going, though it did seem like she was trying to convince herself as she convinced me.

"You'll shoot with Steven Klein. Oh my God, Juergen would love you. So you'll build your book . . . You should sign with Wilhelmina or Boss or—fuck it—let them fight over you! And you'll crash with me, obviously." I was baffled but fully sold.

"Phil! Your life is about to radically change! I'm getting the check. What did you think of the vindaloo?"

The meal might have been delicious, but my attention was elsewhere. I'd never thought of myself as good-looking. I didn't think I was ugly either. I was just . . . there. As Shalom fished out the credit card from her jacket pocket I caught my reflection in the mirrored wall behind her. The humidity made me look more like a librarian who had just taken her hair out of a bun than a male model. But I'd give it a shot. My teachers and my parents were stumped as to what I should do with my life. Shalom had an answer. Sweet relief.

———

Now, a year later, Shalom's predictions had come to pass. I did that test shoot in Toronto. On the morning of the shoot, handwritten directions sat on the passenger seat of the mother ship, a.k.a. my mom's Jetta. They hadn't come easy. The day before, I'd phoned

Marcus, the photographer, handed my mom the receiver, and she'd written down his address. Then my dad had dictated step-by-step instructions that she wrote out in letters so big they resembled the top line of an eye exam chart. My hands tapped at ten and two to a Grateful Dead bootleg: Buffalo '77. I hoped my favorite version of "Franklin's Tower" would calm my nerves.

Marcus lived on the twelfth floor, but I was at the bottom of the fashion industry. He greeted me with enthusiasm. "We have five looks," he said. "Six if we have time for a shirtless portrait."

Please run out of time, I prayed.

"This is Mel. She's doing hair and makeup," Marcus said, introducing a woman with short blond hair and an exposed tribal tattoo on her lower back.

"You weren't lying, Marcus," she said, beaming.

I sat in a kitchen chair with curlers in my hair, wondering what Marcus hadn't lied about.

"You better get used to this, mister," Mel said. "You're going to be working a lot. You have incredible hair and perfect scruff. You must get that all the time."

Quite the contrary: the day before my dad had asked if my barber had died. I couldn't believe how generous they were being. Up until then, I had suspected that Shalom was just being charitable.

I put on a light-gray satin shirt with an oversize collar and posed with my arms crossed above my head, framing my new curls. "Like a young Jim Morrison," Marcus gushed.

This image would appear on the front of my first composite card.

I liked the way I looked in all the clothes, and I even seemed to have a knack for the posing part. We had just enough time to get to all five outfits and not the shirtless portrait. It was the perfect first day.

Now I'd made it to Milan, in the mid-1990s, at the height of a modeling boom. The fashion industry was brimming with female supermodels—Naomi Campbell, Kate Moss, Christy Turlington. Linda Evangelista had stated she wouldn't get out of bed for less than ten thousand dollars a day. And then there was me, living in the Giusti with 120 other dudes, struggling to find a place for ourselves in this world.

We were all first-timers, between the ages of twenty and twenty-eight. I'd expected some culture shock being in Italy, but it wasn't the Italians who took getting used to. I was surrounded by loud sleeveless bros shouting phrases like "Dude, check out how small these fucking coffees are!" and "Have you tried the Italian ice cream? They have more flavors than Baskin-Robbins!" and "This wine is only three dollars American!"

The cadre of models at the Giusti was desperate, viciously competitive, and insecure. One guy, who looked like a hungover Clark Kent, had a taste of glory when he booked an international Calvin Klein campaign. Then the work dried up, and he found himself back in a dormitory fighting for gigs against guys half a decade younger. There were two cousins from Ohio, who lived in the room beneath mine and who both had "hottest guy in their high school" energy. The older of the pair had a chiseled jaw, slicked-back blond hair, and skin fried the color of rust from too many hours under tanning lights. Like Andrew, he felt he owed it to humanity never to wear a shirt. He had done one Versace ad and referred to himself as Mr. Money.

"I've already fucked so many Italian chicks," he boasted on our way to the metro on day two. "They're almost as hot as my girlfriend back home." With his arrogance and Third Reich hairdo, he would have been perfectly cast as the villain in an '80s teen movie. But, like so many who lived at the Giusti, his persona cracked under the slightest inspection.

"He's full of it," his cousin confided to me when Mr. Money had gone off to suntan on the roof. "He's a virgin. He and his girlfriend, who is a born-again virgin, are saving themselves for marriage."

The Giusti housed more than models. The top floors were all low-income housing. Twice a day, a miniature Italian grandmother walked her rabid German shepherd through the halls. The dog went berserk every time it saw anyone; it lunged and snapped its long teeth as its tiny owner tried to restrain it. All she could say in English was "mad dog," at a volume that could barely be heard over the snarling. When the Giusti boys heard her murmuring "mad dog," they scattered, terrified their moisturized skin would be ripped from their perfect bone structure. Aspiring hand models scampered away with their moneymakers jammed deep in their pockets.

As Andrew's roommate, I became an unwilling participant in a constant nutrition seminar. Everything I put in my mouth inspired a monologue. Andrew read the room with the same proficiency with which I read Shakespeare. He lectured me on everything from the fat content of peanuts to the grave importance of drinking three liters of water a day. If I had taken a sip every time he said the word *hydration*, I would have drowned. But there was no escaping him. I needed his help to navigate the city. We'd be walking down the street and a Fiat overflowing with giggling Italian schoolgirls would roll down the window and shout, "Brad Peet! Brad Peet!" He did bear something of a resemblance. With my willowy frame and long dark locks, I could have passed for Angelina Jolie. Andrew and I foreshadowed Brangelina.

I was among people who worked out constantly, applied creams and rectal ointment to their faces, dyed their hair, and restricted their diets to only protein. I'd never been able to put on much muscle and hoped my skinny frame might set me apart from the parade of pointless abs. I thought maybe this was the year that designers were going to say to themselves, "There's nothing worse than a model who looks like a model," the same way in school I'd hoped my teachers would think, "I'm sick of students who can read and write. It's like, enough already." I hoped my weakness would be my strength. But that reversal of misfortune was years away.

Every morning, I arrived at Tino's office, received my go-sees, and headed off to hustle around the city to meet designers. I traveled with the herd of male models, mortified by their public feats of strength but grateful for their ability to read street signs, call sheets, and maps. We waited at castings together and presented our books to designers and stylists, hoping for their approval but mostly receiving their rejection. Usually, they took one look at my book and simply said "Grazie." *Grazie* translated to "none for me, thanks."

At go-sees, I pined for any justification for being so far from home and so uncomfortable in my current situation. Any special attention from a designer gave me a spike in optimism. Being asked to put on a sport coat felt like a victory and, though I hated being shirtless, being asked to take my shirt off was suddenly an honor. The fashion industry and I had all the trademarks of an abusive relationship. Designers looked me up and down with the subtlety of a judge at the Westminster Dog Show. Soon, I got accustomed to being poked, prodded, and moved around like a piece of furniture. I was trusted to do nothing, from tucking in my shirt to adjusting my manhood.

I looked around at my fellow models, muscled jocks who now were spun around and tussled about by small gay men—the type of men they must've bullied back home—now becoming putty in their hands. Steve and Tommy's older brother James had been the only person brave enough to be openly gay in Oshawa. He wore a beret instead of a beanie in the winter. I admired that he took pride in his appearance and tended to his bonsai tree. In Milan, gay men were in charge. I loved this inversion.

Yet the thing that remained the same in Italy was that I felt alienated. Back home, I was in over my head in the classroom. Now I felt that way at Tino's agency, at castings, and at the Giusti. I didn't fit in. What dyslexia was to reading, my physique was to men's fashion.

3

Sick Chicken

My second Saturday in Italy, Tino told me discotheque promoters would pay models to dance shirtless on top of speakers in their clubs. Dancing for dollars, they called it. I was on the fence. Just the summer before, I had been too shy to take my shirt off at a pool party. I'd bribed my friend Joshua with a king can of beer to push me in while I was clothed so I could splash around with everyone shamelessly. I knew Andrew had danced for dollars the weekend before, so I asked his advice.

"Getting paid to do what I would probably be doing anyway?" Andrew scoffed as he squeezed into an undershirt that fit him like a sausage casing. "Italian chicks worship American guys. Why would you deprive them of that? Why would you deprive yourself?"

"It feels sleazy," I said.

"Sleazy? Last week an old Italian chick tucked fifty thousand lire down the front of my pants. My only advice is the more you show the more you make."

I gulped. I felt this whole thing was a giant mistake. What was

I thinking, flying halfway around the world to be a model? Andrew interrupted my regret spiral.

"I fucking hate that people associate booty shorts exclusively with gay dudes." He stared at himself in the mirror with a troubled expression as he rolled up his gym shorts to reveal freshly squat-walked quads.

We joined Mr. Money, his cousin, and one other model on the street outside the Giusti, piled into a tiny Fiat station wagon, and were driven by a promoter to a discotheque in the outskirts of Milan. The owner eyed us as we climbed out of the car. In a thick Italian accent, he said "nice" as each model revealed himself. I got out last. He was silent. I told myself that being speechless is often a good thing.

"I want you dancing up on the speakers," he told us. "No shirts. Very sexy. If you have fun, my customers have fun."

I looked over at Andrew. He was already topless and clearly in the zone. I was wearing brown cords and a vintage dress shirt, which I nervously began to unbutton.

"Except you," the owner snapped at me. "You just stand by the bar." I understood his disappointment. He wanted Chippendales, and a dude from Soundgarden showed up. By this point, I was so used to my body being rejected that I just nodded and followed Andrew's muscles into the club.

Besides the staff, we were the first to arrive. But that didn't stop the smoke machines from billowing out or the strobe lights from illuminating the club. The rest of the models assumed their positions on the speakers that towered over the dance floor. I leaned against a copper-top bar that reflected the lights, which combined with the Eurobeat to create a hellscape-like atmosphere. The club filled up, and Andrew's speaker was by far the most popular. Women faced him, dancing and cheering, as he gyrated to the music.

One of the bartenders took pity on me and kept feeding me drinks. He was the only person who acknowledged my existence that night. The women contemplating scaling the speakers looked right through me. It was beyond emasculating. It reminded me of the seventh-grade trip I took to Barbados with my family. My sister and I snuck out of our hotel one night and went to an outdoor bar. I had long hair and was approached by a middle-aged local who asked me if I wanted to dance. Sensing there was a major misunderstanding occurring, I said, "I'm a guy." He took a minute to compute the information, then, in his thick Bajan accent, asked if I was gay.

———

In late June, as the number of castings ramped up and the shows drew closer, the Giusti boys shifted into high gear. Push-up sessions became as ritualistic and frequent as Muslim prayer. Attitudes intensified and grew more elaborate. Successful male models took on fake personas like professional wrestlers. The industry wanted the character Hulk Hogan, not the person Terry Bollea. There were the twins from New York who dressed like Donnie Brasco, the tortured bookworm who always had a Dostoevsky novel under his arm, two rival Tibetan monks who hated each other, and a guy

I'd met through Shalom who suddenly revamped his look to something I can only describe as "friend of Johnny Depp."

I too wanted to emerge from the persona cocoon and reveal myself as a more bookable butterfly. I just couldn't, the same way I can't spell *appreciate* or feel comfortable watching a condom commercial with my mom. I would pose, but not in that way. Much of my identity came from being sincere. I grew up in a town where if you wore a band's T-shirt, you were promptly asked to name three songs. That was the environment. Reinventing yourself was not an option. You were expected to support the same hockey team from the cradle to the grave. If someone wore Doc Martens boots and wasn't considered an official skinhead or rude boy, they'd have them removed and be forced to walk home from the bus stop in their socks. I never once wore a Grateful Dead shirt until I attended one of their shows. Now I was among the finest posers in the world in that same Grateful Dead T-shirt.

Earnestness felt as debilitating in the fashion industry as illiteracy was in school. I desperately wanted my first booking, so I turned to prayer, something I hadn't done since my problems started in school and I tried to pray away my disability. In between castings I would leave the pack and go to the Duomo, the second-largest cathedral in the world, located in the middle of Milan. Tourists would also make the pilgrimage, kneeling in front of the pews and praying for traditional things like strength, forgiveness, and Nana's speedy recovery after her gallbladder surgery. I'm sure God rolled His eyes when I requested that Gianni Versace like me. And could He make the clothes at the Gucci casting fit? I pictured our Lord and Savior with a tape measure hung over His shoulders and a pushpin in His mouth, telling Moses, "I haven't altered slacks in an eternity."

I made many trips to the pay phone in the lobby to try to locate Shalom as she globe-trotted, shooting with the world's most famous photographers. I hoped she could offer me pointers on surviving in this surreal world. I knew deep down the only modeling advice she could offer was "look as remarkable as me." I eventually settled for a conversation with her assistant Bradley, who advised, "Be yourself, you're fierce." Heading back to my room, hearing barks and mutters of "mad dog," I questioned whether talking to Shalom's assistant was worth risking getting mauled by a German shepherd.

I got into the habit of going for walks at night to get a break from the vibe at the Giusti. One muggy night, I returned from the piazza to find our room filled with smoke and the sounds of sizzling flesh. Andrew and Mr. Money toiled shirtless over the stovetop, flipping and prodding large cubes of meat.

"You'll never guess what we're cooking," Mr. Money said to me over his shoulder.

"Horse," Andrew answered, implying he didn't have the patience to hear my laundry list of incorrect animals. He was right: my hunch wasn't "horse," just like if he'd asked me to guess how we were getting to the airport my first response wouldn't have been "Zamboni."

Andrew and Mr. Money were the first to consume the glorious beasts, but it became an overnight sensation because it was higher in protein and lower in fat than beef. The horse meat plug was an old Italian man who sold his wares out of a dilapidated trailer parked at a nearby piazza. I had walked past it several times and thought it was abandoned. Now business was booming, with a long line of Giustonias commenting, "I like that it's chewy, it's like we're burning calories as we eat" and "Native Americans ate it and I hear that's the direction Missoni is going this season."

One evening as I accompanied Andrew to pick up his meat, I was horrified to see that the old man had decorated the interior of his trailer with photos of majestic steeds galloping across the Italian countryside. The decor made me think of a serial killer who celebrates his kills by making jewelry out of his victim's bones. Which I had heard was the direction Alexander McQueen was heading that season.

I kept that observation to myself, not wanting to stomach another bomb. None of my jokes, my attempts at connection, had broken through to the other models. I understood being professional and wanting to be successful. I wanted it badly. But pretending the whole thing wasn't a ridiculous facade was too much to bear. We were grown men competing in a beauty pageant. How could no one else see the irony of trying to be the manliest in the hopes of also being the belle of the ball? I was surrounded by so many things to mock and had no one to mock them with. I couldn't understand how people could take themselves so seriously. I'd crack a joke, and the other models, the ones who had dedicated themselves to the gym and the craft of wearing other people's pants professionally, would look at me like, "Why are you ruining this for us?" It's one thing to be lonely when you're by yourself. It's far more soul-crushing to be surrounded by others and still feel absolutely isolated.

After all, we were male models, second-class citizens in the fashion industry. Instead of raking in cash like our female counterparts, we were often paid in clothes. I felt paying a model in clothes was like paying a dishwasher in dirty dishes. I once took a hundred-pound voucher I'd received to an AllSaints store and sold it for fifty pounds to a guy standing in line. When you're a model, you are the product that you are pushing, so when endless people pass it's hard not to take it personally. Any positive response becomes monumental. A slight nod from a designer was a triumph. Being asked to walk felt like being knighted by the queen. I was looking for any indication that I had made the right decision in coming to Milan.

As Fashion Week approached, none seemed forthcoming. I had exaggerated my measurements on my composite card to those I'd thought would make me appear a more bookable "model size." This backfired. I was far too thin for most of the clothes they were bringing me to potentially wear. Versace said "grazie." Valentino complimented me on my green vintage shirt but . . . grazie. Gucci, Balenciaga, Costume National. Grazie, grazie, grazie. After a day full of grazies, I associated the word with defeat. When a baker said "grazie" after I bought bread from him on my way back to the Giusti, my first thought was, are you fucking saying I'm too skinny to buy a baguette? Back at our room Andrew told me not to worry, no one was skinny enough to justify eating carbs.

No one booked me or took much interest. And then I saw Armani.

Giorgio Armani's casting was the biggest go-see in Milan. The one everyone waited for. We arrived at his compound in the center of the Brera District—a marble, museum-like structure a stone's throw from the Duomo where I had been badgering God on a daily basis with my superficial requests. Security at the gate allowed in a hundred or so men at a time. When it was my group's turn, we were ushered into a vast, light-filled atrium. We headed down a giant marble staircase that opened out to the famous auditorium where most of Armani's fashion shows took place. Rows of white leather seats surrounded an illuminated runway.

My group of horse meat–filled models walked alongside the runway and sat opposite Armani and his entourage. Giorgio Armani was the most famous fashion designer in the world. The Armani suit had become synonymous with men's fashion. His taste was timeless and displayed extreme self-discipline. For a young wannabe male model, to walk for him was a huge opportunity and a potential game changer. I looked across to him as he sat, regal and expressionless, his white hair outdone by his even whiter teeth and contrasting with a tan that looked too dark to be healthy.

They called one name at a time. Seventy guys walked before me. One did a backflip when he reached the end of the runway, and everyone cheered. For some, just to walk the hallowed runway at the casting was accomplishment enough. Out of my group, about a dozen were asked to don a sport coat, and a dozen got to take off their shirts. When one model bared his slight belly, Armani said something in Italian to his assistants, who chuckled.

"Armani says you ate too much pasta," another assistant translated loudly. The whole auditorium erupted.

When my turn came, I walked up and down the runway.

Armani looked at my composite card and told me to try on one of the sports jackets and walk again. As I took off the jacket, he said, "Grazie."

Armani's grazie didn't sting too badly. If I had removed my shirt and Armani had quipped "not enough pasta," it would have crushed with the spectators and driven home my shortcomings. I took pride in the fact that I was part of the elite group that was asked to try on a jacket. My ego was surviving on scraps.

It began to dawn on me that the models in Milan were willing participants in a giant scam. The agencies made money off everything we did. They got a cut of the accommodations, test shoots, the printing of composite cards, *and* 20 percent of any actual modeling work. Suddenly being invited to model in Europe didn't feel so prestigious. The more models, the more money, as far as agencies were concerned. This realization made me feel even more insecure.

Among the biggest scams were clubs and after-parties. Promoters were also bitten by the persona bug. They all wore attention-grabbing garb. One had a whole urban matador thing going on—bolero-cut jackets, slicked-back hair, and a bright-red scooter that would trigger any bull. He would offer us tickets to his events and encourage us to invite female models. Once we arrived, we, like a bull stabbed by a matador, learned we had been deceived. He and the other promoters would quickly whisk the female models off to the VIP section to be wooed by sultans, shipping tycoons, and Leonardo DiCaprio. They used us to fill the dance floor and remind the people in the roped-off area that they were the chosen ones. The male models who brought the most girls were rewarded with drink tickets, which was a real incentive because they inflated drink prices so much that for the average model they were completely out of reach.

Guys treated these parties like go-sees. Anything to achieve an edge, to stand out from the crowd. They weren't being phony for the sake of being phony; it was strategic. I realized the designers wanted these characters, these faux rock stars. My authenticity hadn't landed me any auditions.

Then one afternoon I headed to the agency, and a group of models hanging out by the stairs parted for me. When I reached the office Tino jumped up from his desk yelling, "Ciao, bella Canadese! You booked Armani!" He hugged me and kissed both my cheeks. "Molto bene! You got to go to the fitting!"

Shocked, I headed back to Armani's compound. Booking Armani felt like the first win I could remember since the party I attended for my hockey team when I was eight. My name was drawn first for the raffle, which meant I got to pick first from the folding card table of prizes. As I headed to the front of the room, I heard my coach say, "I wonder what he'll pick." But he was clearly being facetious. Everyone knew I was heading straight to the big-ticket item: a digital watch with a built-in AM radio and a head-phone jack. It became my prized possession and started my lifelong love of watches.

At Armani, I gave my name to security. The fact that it now appeared on a much shorter list filled me with pride. I made my way down that marble staircase that had seemed so intimidating just a few days before. Now each step felt like a mini victory lap.

Backstage, I came to a rack of clothes with my headshot displayed on the end. A young Italian fashion student named Elena handed me a watch and said, "A gift from Mr. Armani." A watch. Maybe destiny was a real thing. Maybe everything happened for a reason. Maybe not being able to read, the humiliation of special ed, the endless hours of drudgery dealing with consonants and vowels at the kitchen table with my mom—maybe all of it had led to this moment.

Elena said, "Outfit one," and started grabbing clothes off hangers. My heart sank when I saw the pants. They looked enormous. I hoped my depth perception was malfunctioning, a symptom of dyslexia. I slid into the pants with alarming ease. The only contact I experienced with the silk-wool blend was where they pooled at my feet. I tried to convince myself that this was the style. Maybe Armani had drawn inspiration this season from children playing dress-up in their dad's clothes.

Elena's sudden stress levels made it clear that wasn't the case. She frantically tried to adjust the belt. Even on the last hole, the waist hovered around me like a hula hoop. Next came the shirt, a mesh tank top that fit me like a woman's beach cover-up. The bottom rested just above my knees. Then on came the collarless sport coat. I was swimming in it. When Elena pulled it forward, it enveloped my shoulders. It looked like I was peering out from behind a giant set of curtains. Even the sunglasses were too big for my head.

Elena looked baffled. She spoke Italian frantically into her headset. I was hoping she was requesting another size. Anything but another model. Then she told me, "Mr. Armani want see you."

I stepped out from backstage and onto a series of illuminated panels that made up the runway. Armani and his team sat in the same positions as they had during my audition. They seemed miles away. As I walked, I began to feel my pants pulled down by the weight of the belt. I had no choice but to clutch them with a sweaty hand. I tried to maintain my pace, hoping they'd think it was a stylistic choice. I could hear the group snickering as I approached. I stood momentarily before Armani motioned for me to leave.

Backstage, I flung off the jacket, released my grip on the belt, and let gravity do the work. Figuring that was it, I started putting on my clothes. Elena held out her hand for me to stop while listening to instructions coming through her headset. "Outfit two," she said.

Three more outfits, each as ill-fitting as the last, and three more long illuminated walks followed, each met with more snickering and Italian wisecracks. The last was nothing more than a pair of leather sandals that fit me like flippers and a speedo that, on me, defied the properties of spandex. The elasticity refused to register on my underdeveloped midsection.

To add to the humiliation, Elena accompanied me this time. We stood together as Armani laughed so hard that he had to wipe away tears. When he was able to take a breath, he made quips in Italian that his entourage found very humorous.

Elena and I returned backstage silently. I started stripping out of my speedo and asked, "What was Armani saying?" I knew perfectly well I wouldn't like the answer.

Elena took a long moment to make sure she was translating accurately. "He called you sick chicken."

I could tell that we both felt the assessment was about right. I dressed, said "ciao," and handed her back the watch. I could have easily slipped it into my pocket, and no one would have noticed. But it would have haunted me. The watch symbolized yet another time I wasn't good enough. But unlike in school, I knew I was on the right track.

Defeated, I took the metro back to the Giusti. I misread the map and got off at the wrong stop. As I emerged from the platform, I spotted a gaggle of prostitutas in oversize furs flashing cars. One of them turned to me and opened her coat. Below a pair of massive breasts swung the largest penis I'd ever seen in my life. She looked like she had been drawn by a cartoonist at an adults-only theme park. I'd never seen a person like this before. Instead of shock, I felt envy. She could have really filled out Armani's speedo.

My genetics were the ultimate obstacle, just like they had been in school. In Oshawa, I was surrounded by people who were phonically proficient. In Milan, I was competing head-to-head with the best-looking people in the world. Back then, I was awestruck by Trudy Nickerson's ability to get ten out of ten on a spelling test. Now I marveled at my colleagues' perfect bodies. Literally the ones you see in magazines. Entering first grade brought to my attention my learning disability; losing Armani confirmed my physical shortcomings. Both were things I couldn't change.

If I'd ever felt decent about the way I looked, my time in Milan threatened to ruin that. It was as if someone said, "Let's take this thing you're neutral about and make it your livelihood." In modeling, you are the product being sold. You take constant self-inventory. You know things have gone awry when your grudge with God goes beyond the lousy job he did on your calves, and you find yourself thinking, I hate my clavicle.

That night I returned to the Giusti, back to the smell of freshly seared horse meat. The whole place smelled like a Ponderosa. Mr. Money made sure everyone knew he'd booked Versace. His cousin got Balenciaga. But for most at the Giusti, determination was turning to desperation. Rejection this season meant returning to college to reclaim their status as the most gorgeous guy on campus.

———

I was too skinny for Armani's clothes that season. But not for Dolce & Gabbana's. At the D&G casting, I saw other guys with pale skin, long hair, bony bodies, and angular faces. They booked me immediately. I still had no clue what the guy at the Giusti meant that first day when he told me I had a Dolce & Gabbana attitude, but I did seem to check all the other D&G boxes. I caught another break when I landed Dries Van Noten, but that felt like a small victory. He hired three times as many models as most designers. This included Andrew; our contrasting appearances proved Dries Van Noten was casting a wide net.

I arrived super early at a nondescript warehouse located at one of the last stops on the metro. I was directed to go in through the back entrance. Inside it was already packed with models, dressers, and makeup artists. Dolce and Gabbana looked impeccable as they presided over the madness. An assistant checked off my name and took me to my rack, where I was instructed to change into tighty whities and an undershirt bearing the D&G logo. Unfortunately, I had to get changed right there in front of everyone. But as the other models stripped down, I couldn't believe my eyes. Most of them were as scrawny as me. I immediately wanted to grab each one and quickly quiz them to see if they also misspelled *apparently*.

Once we were in our matching undergarments, everyone was sent to hair and makeup. We made our way to the makeup chairs like an undernourished Ken doll assembly line. My hair was flat-ironed. Foundation was applied to my face, neck, and upper chest. In the mirror, I saw something that resembled a model looking back at me for the first time. My moment of achievement was short-lived. I spilled pasta salad from catering on the undershirt and had to beg for another one.

Someone called "first outfits." It was like an alarm had gone off at a firehouse. In a matter of seconds I was dressed, rushed into line, and pushed onto the runway. The speakers blared Blur's "Song 2," and I began pretending I knew what I was doing. A couple meters away, a wall of flashing cameras seemed to be stacked on top of each other like an art installation. I hadn't thought about what I would do when I reached the runway's end. I just knew I had to do something. Suddenly I remembered Shalom's assistant's advice to "be fierce." I posed with my hands on my hips and leaned to the side, an unprecedented move for a male model. Shockingly, I heard applause as the cameras snapped. The picture would appear in the collection catalog that showcased the fashion shows from that season. My parents drove to Toronto and bought it at an international magazine store for sixty dollars.

A few days later, Andrew and I hopped on a bus full of models headed to Florence to walk for Dries Van Noten. We walked from the bus stop, past little porchetteria stands hawking sandwiches, to a massive public park called Piazzale Michelangelo. I stared up at a giant bronze replica of the statue of David. A crowd had assembled around the base of a long catwalk. As I followed Andrew through the throng, I couldn't tell who were models and who were just lunatics who had wandered in off the street.

It didn't seem to make much difference to the showrunners. I was hurriedly clad in baggy straight-legged pants and a blue linen knit sweater. As the show started, models were encouraged to talk to each other and interact with spectators. Some of the crowd joined the show and walked alongside us. Hardly the formalities that had taken place at Armani's compound and a welcome relief from the rigid hierarchies of Fashion Week. The show ended with a grand fireworks display.

After the finale, the models and spectators mixed together at a wild after-party. Dries Van Noten provided food and booze and gave each model a T-shirt as a souvenir. My mom still has mine, preserved immaculately with the rest of my modeling memorabilia. It was the first time I had let loose since I had arrived in Italy. It might have been the red wine I was consuming directly from the bottle, but hanging with models when they weren't competing for shows or to see who could get the most lira stuffed down their pants wasn't so bad.

As I sipped wine, I spotted a woman with a pixie haircut, dressed in all black. I pointed her out to Andrew and proclaimed,

"That's the prettiest girl in Italy." When he replied, "She looks like a dude," I knew I had to introduce myself. Isabella was an art student. When all the other models drunkenly loaded on the bus to head back to Milan, she snuck me into her family's apartment. We fooled around quietly in her living room while her sister slept in the next room.

After, she handed me a carefully drawn map to the train station. I kissed her goodbye and walked the cobblestone streets of Florence as the sun came up. I felt incredible. Each miniature Fiat I passed reminded me that I had made it out of Oshawa, worlds away from its shitty dustbuster minivans.

I took the train back to Milan and found the Giusti quiet and empty. People had started trickling out the day after the last show. Hungover Clark Kent sat on the floor in the hall.

"I didn't book shit. Nothing," he said without looking up.

I felt guilty for feeling so good about the last twenty hours and tried to console him. "Dude, this business is so unpredictable. Probably means you'll clean up next season."

"Fuck it, I'm done. I guess I'll put my law degree to work."

I was in disbelief. I couldn't get my head around anyone who could read going through this, yet alone a lawyer. "Could be worse. You could be a fucking model," I said.

He looked up from his lap and laughed. Finally, someone got one of my jokes!

I'd decided to fly to London at the recommendation of my agents. "Canadese, you will be back," Tino proclaimed. "You book

Armani next year." Andrew told me he was staying on to shoot some editorials, but I suspected he'd be dancing for dollars.

"Well, man," I told Andrew. "Good luck with everything. I'll see you down the road."

"Right on," he said. "I'll be back here for winter. You?"

"We'll see," I said. "Keep an eye out for me on the call sheets, I guess."

"Sure. Oh, by the way, I'm changing my name. It's Eden now. Like the garden."

"Yeah, I'm not gonna call you that."

Shalom had been right: my life had radically changed. I was out of Oshawa. That summer in Milan taught me to focus on things I can control. As a model, I showed up and hoped for the best. When it came to my input, less was more. This gave me a lot of time to observe the people around me, people who didn't embrace the philosophy "Life's a bitch and then you die." I realized I wanted to take my dad's work ethic and apply it to a job I loved, where the more I put into it, the more I got out of it.

I experienced more during a few weeks in Milan than I could have in a lifetime in Oshawa. Before Shalom opened up this world for me, I had been stuck. Now I was in motion. Modeling wasn't my goal, but it was leading me somewhere. Being directionless is only a bad thing if you let it prevent you from moving.

4

Old World Charm

When I was a kid, I was desperate for people to see me as anything but a special ed student. I tried to conceal my dyslexia from the world the way one hides a hickey from their parents at the breakfast table. I attempted to use my appearance to distract from my learning difference. So, when I developed a love for Bob Marley at age eleven, I decided to grow dreadlocks. They would be the perfect smokescreen. When a white person has dreads, no one wonders what else is wrong with them.

Dreadlocks proved more of a challenge for my bone-straight hair than reading was for my dyslexic brain. I twisted gel into clumps of my hair, which left me with a Jheri curl. I wanted Peter Tosh, and I got Rick James. Next, I washed my hair with a bar of soap and didn't rinse it. This produced dull ringlets. I looked more like a forefather than a Rastafarian.

My dreadful quest ended when I discovered "rude boys," the multiracial ska and reggae–loving subculture that started in Jamaica in the '60s and was revived in the late '70s in England by bands like The Specials, Madness, and The Selector. Rude boys had shaved heads and flattops. They rocked zoot suits formally and Fred Perry tennis shirts casually. I embraced this culture and was rarely seen without the "rudiest of the rude" Doc Martens and wraparound sunglasses.

When I left school, I stopped using my appearance to mask my learning difference. But I felt like I had come full circle when I arrived at a car park in the north London neighborhood of Tufnell Park for my first editorial shoot in England. In the boot of the photographer's Peugeot, the stylist had laid out my dream wardrobe from my rude boy days. The gig was for *More*, the first of many teeny-bopper magazines I shot for when I arrived in London. The type of magazine my sister read when I was too young to know reading for pleasure would never be an option.

The stylist introduced me to Cara, a model with a pixie haircut. When I went to shake her hand, Cara came in for a hug. "We might as well get it out of the way," she said. "I have a feeling we're going to be snogging all day."

Moments later, Cara stripped down to her underwear. I haltingly stepped out of my jeans. I stood on top of my desert boots, shivering in my boxer briefs and wishing the stylist would decide which shade of khaki pants matched my Fred Perry polo. I kept my eyes forward while Cara assessed my physique.

"I would kill for your legs," she said, stretching her arms behind her back.

Cara was right—our first shot called for snogging. The photographer, whose mission statement seemed to be "shot first, safety second," made us kiss in the middle of the street. When the light changed, we sprinted to the curb, Cara's hand in mine. "Warm me up, love," she told me. I hugged her as if we were slow dancing at a wedding. Maybe this is how we'll dance at our wedding, I thought.

The next shot's location was in front of a brightly painted chip shop. We were instructed to eat a french fry—or a chip, as the love of my life called it—from each end and meet in the middle à la *Lady and the Tramp.*

"Do you want to come around to mine for tea, then?" Cara asked as we changed into our final outfits of the day. "I live a couple stops away on the Tube in Camden."

"Sure," I said.

Just then, the photographer's friend pulled up on a Vespa. "You two lovebirds drive off into the sunset," the photographer instructed. Cara and I hopped on. She wrapped her arms around me, shifting her weight against my back. After a couple takes of us whizzing up and down the street, he shouted, "Brilliant. We got it."

I parked the scooter and held my future wife's hand as she stepped to the curb. I thought about us telling people our origin story. "You tell it, babe. I love the way you say it," Cara would say at a dinner party at a posh flat in Notting Hill.

"Okay, but then we should go," I'd concede with a sigh. "We promised the sitter we wouldn't be too late. Young Bobby and Jerry have school tomorrow."

"You just got here," Stella McCartney would protest. "Dad is going to be gutted he missed you guys again."

I snapped out of my daydream when Cara grabbed the scooter

keys out of my hand. "Give us a go then," she said. She hit the gas and popped the clutch. The Vespa took off, rising on its rear wheel and bucking her off. Cara landed on her feet. The scooter slid on its side, scraping across the asphalt.

The Vespa's owner ran toward us, screaming, "What the fuck, you dizzy slag?"

Cara hit me with a look that said, "You're going to let him talk to me like that?" I didn't know a slag from a snog, but suggested he calm down.

"You can't control your fucking bird, mate?" he shouted in my face.

The stylist stepped in and ferried us back to the Peugeot. As we changed, Cara plugged a pair of headphones into her ears.

"Ready for tea?" I asked.

Cara removed only one of her headphones. "I'm going to head home on my own, mate."

Instead of going home with a model, I headed back to Mrs. O'Connor's. Mrs. O'Connor was a miniature woman in her late sixties. She ran a boarding house out of her council estate town house in Clapton, a rough neighborhood in the East London borough of Hackney. The rent was fifty pounds a week, which included room and board.

I was the only guest. The only evidence another boarder had stayed there was that Mrs. O'Connor sometimes referenced a guy named Van. Whenever she mentioned his name, she blessed herself.

I assumed Van had died until Mrs. O'Connor told me it was to "help him find his way."

I'd arrived in Clapton on a January afternoon three weeks before the *More* shoot. Mrs. O'Connor opened her door and peered up at me from behind thick glasses nestled beneath a bowl cut. "There you are," she said, then ripped my transatlantic suitcase out of my hand and began charging up the stairs. Like an ant, she could carry objects many times her weight. I followed her into her spotless home. Not one lace doily was out of place.

Ascending the stairs, Mrs. O'Connor gave me a who's who of the photographs that lined the walls. Her son, Noah, "who taught English in Prague." Her sister, "may she rest in peace." She nodded toward a gruesome picture of Jesus Christ on the cross and said, "I hope he needs no introduction." Her tone implied he needed an introduction, as if she suspected my suitcase was filled with satanic paraphernalia, and if she opened it, goat heads and pentagrams would spill out.

At my room, Mrs. O'Connor flung my suitcase on the single bed. She pointed to a cupboard with a bike lock wrapped around the handles. "That's my son's and shouldn't be fussed with." She clapped her little hands, commanded me to "get settled," and zipped out of the room. I sat on the bed, dehydrated and jet-lagged.

Downstairs, I found Mrs. O'Connor bustling around in the kitchen. She called out, "Hope you're hungry tonight. We're having chicken."

"Great," I replied. "Is there a convenience store nearby?"

"A what?"

"Just a place where I could buy a bottle of water?"

"There's a corner shop by the chippies. But why in the world would anyone buy water? We have all the water you need right here," she said, turning on the faucet for effect.

"I just want some fresh air," I said, beelining for the door.

"Are you planning on paying for that too?" she shouted over the sound of the water.

Outside, I was surrounded by redbrick town houses, identical except for their window coverings. Although lace was hands down the most popular. I bought a bottle of water at the corner store, knowing I'd best drink it before I returned or suffer the same fate as Jesus. Leaning on an ancient stone wall, I considered the logistics of returning home. I was homesick and worried about my friend Cam.

The weekend before I moved to England, my Canadian friends threw me a going-away party in Toronto. Cam and I continued festivities the next night, drinking at a club called the Left Bank. After many jack and gingers, I left Cam to use the bathroom, located down a steep staircase. When I left the bathroom, I saw a group of people at the bottom of the stairs. I felt sick in the pit of my stomach. I squeezed through the crowd and saw Cam lying on the ground, unconscious. Paramedics appeared, loaded Cam on a stretcher, carried him up the stairs, and wheeled him into an ambulance.

At the emergency room, I found Cam semiconscious but completely aware of what was happening. He was harnessed tightly to the stretcher. He couldn't move his head or limbs. "Phil, this isn't funny!" he shouted. "Untie me Phil please, please Phil."

I pleaded with Cam to calm down. He screamed for me to help him for hours. Eventually, I curled up on the floor, using my oversize chain wallet as a pillow. I woke up when an orderly kicked my foot. "They're admitting him," he said.

Cam had a severe concussion. The hospital released him the day before I left for England. I visited Cam at his parents' house in Oshawa and we shuffled to the bottom of the driveway. "This is the most I've exerted myself since the accident," he said. Back inside, I took off his slip-on shoes and helped him back onto the couch. I had no idea if he would ever recover. I blamed dyslexia for Cam's injury. If I hadn't been a model, I wouldn't have had a going-away party in the first place. And I was only modeling because I couldn't read well enough to attend college.

My guilt spiral was interrupted by a guy running down the street as fast as his baggy jeans allowed. Every few steps, he hiked them up with one hand. Another man chased at his heels, brandishing a metal pole. The type of pole you see holding up a chain-link fence. Or use to persuade someone to pay off a debt. The two men disappeared around the other side of the store.

That night, Mrs. O'Connor cooked chicken as promised. After dinner, she placed the carcass in a Pyrex mixing bowl on the counter and threw a tea towel over it. I asked if I could put the leftovers in the fridge.

"What are you on about?" she shot back.

I thought I was on a streak of not having salmonella.

———

The next morning, Mrs. O'Connor had her friend Louise over for tea. Louise brought along King, a giant Doberman pinscher who appeared to be the same age as Mrs. O'Connor. King had cancer and had lost the ability to walk, stand, or do most dog-related activities. He lay on the floor with a diaper wrapped around his haunches. When I entered the kitchen, King had a conniption. He wormed toward me, trying to maul my ankles as I poured a bowl of muesli from the ziplock bag my mom had packed for me, which Mrs. O'Connor called bird feed. When King got within striking distance, Louise pulled him back. He started his conquest all over again.

I had an appointment at my new modeling agency, Nuff Said. They specialized in nontraditional-looking models. Pugs called us "just your face" models. At Nuff Said's office in Chelsea, I met the head of the agency, Victoria. She was a former model and still had the slight figure, all-black outfit, and omnipresent cigarette in her mouth to prove it.

"Darling," she said. "Let's go meet the team, darling."

Victoria took me to meet the other agents. We found her boyfriend with his feet up on a round desk that reminded me of Tino's, marking his territory with white Adidas. I would learn that these shoes were the mark of drug dealers in England. "White trainers, white powder," a friend would say. And it was true—Victoria's boyfriend would go on to be arrested in one of the biggest coke busts in British history.

Before I left, Victoria gave me a day pass to Jubilee Hall, a gym in Covent Garden. Later that day, as I did the standard model chest, biceps, and abs workout, I noticed primarily gay men on the gym floor. Fewer meatheads than at a straight gym suited me fine. I felt as out of place in a gym as in a bookstore. After my workout, I stopped at the gym's café. I gazed at the fresh salads in a deli case. A hand-drawn sign advertised "three-pound," "four-pound," and "five-pound" plates of food.

"How much is the three-pound plate?" I asked the guy behind the counter, who was handsome and in his late twenties. His upper body filled out his black T-shirt perfectly. He even made his black apron look as stylish as the expensive clothes I hoped to wear for a living.

He flashed a broad smile. His white teeth popped against the golden glow of his skin, which, in England, meant he was no stranger to a sunbed. "Three pounds, mate," he replied in a cockney accent.

"What about the four-pound plate?" I asked.

"Four pounds, mate."

"How about the five?"

"It costs five pounds," he replied with a perplexed expression.

"I'll go with the five-pound plate, please."

"Where are you from?" he asked as he placed a piece of pesto chicken beside my pasta salad.

"Oshawa, Ontario."

"Canada, cool beans. Oshawa," he repeated. "I love that word. It sounds beautiful."

An image popped into my head of a tire fire set by disgruntled factory workers in front of the old GM plant on Ritson Road.

"Oshawa is like Detroit minus the European flare," I said.

He laughed. "I've been to Detroit, mate," he said, handing over my plate.

It felt good to make someone laugh. I headed to a table between the counter and the locker rooms. I was chewing on steamed broccoli when I jumped up and ran back to the counter.

"Dude, I can't believe I just did that. I'm an idiot," I said. "I saw pounds and thought it meant weight. I forgot that's what you guys call money."

"You're all right, mate," the guy replied when I stopped to breathe. "Just thought you were taking the piss," he said. "I'm Ronnie, by the way."

"I'm Phil." We shook hands, and I noticed his vintage Rolex. "I love your 1016."

"You know your watches," he said, rubbing the crystal against his T-shirt.

"I know Rolex. 1016s are one of my grails. Why were you in Detroit?"

"My ex and I drove across the States. We went everywhere. It was amazing. We wanted to go to Canada but didn't make it up there." Ronnie paused. "Wait, it's up, isn't it?"

I nodded.

"We started in Detroit. You lot drive on the other side, don't you? I almost drove through a zebra crossing. You call it something different over there?"

"A crosswalk?"

"Oh, right, a crosswalk," Ronnie said. "I stopped at the last second. There was this older bloke with a long gray beard. He looked like an old-timey American prospector. I rolled down the window and said, 'Excuse me, sir. I'm really sorry.' The geezer spins around, gives me the finger with both hands, and shouts, 'Eat shit and die, fucker!'"

By the time I stopped laughing, I knew we would be friends.

––––––––––

Ronnie grew up in East London with a view of the Blackfriars Bridge from his flat. His family was very working class. His father grew up so impoverished that he and his brothers made a living as street fighters. They had bones removed from their noses so they'd never break in a bout.

Everything Ronnie owned was museum worthy. If he wore Levi's, they were produced on denim looms in the 1950s. His Adidas Superstars were from the '70s. In his cashmere sweater collection, he prided himself on having every shade of every color. He loved gifting treasures from his archives, but if you wanted a blue jumper, you needed to be very specific about the hue. He collected foam Disney toys from the '50s, purchased from antique markets in the mornings on his way home from long nights out.

One night, we walked home from the Prince Bonaparte, a pub where we hung out and Ronnie picked up the odd shift. He knelt on the steps of a town house and cut two lines of coke. Always a gentleman, he let me go first. As he was snorting his own, the door rattled. From the click of the lock to the opening of the door, Ronnie finished his line, sprang to his feet, wiped the remaining coke against his gums, and greeted the woman. "You're not Stanley!" he exclaimed. "Oh wait, what? We're at the wrong place. Philip, this isn't Annabelle's flat! Have a wonderful evening." On the Tube, Ronnie would riffle a businessman's hair and get his hand back on the pole before his victim took his eyes off his paper. His quick wit and limbs let him escape any situation and made me die of laughter while watching him.

Ronnie told me about the Iron Bar, a new gay bar in Soho that was hiring. "It used to be called Freddie's, an absolute legend place where we used to get off our faces. You would have loved it, Phyllis," he explained. He passed along the number of the manager, an Austrian part-time model named Manfred. I loved the idea of working at a gay bar in England. It was such an un-Oshawa thing to do. I planned to tell Manfred I was a hard worker and a quick learner. That was only half a lie. I'm the world's slowest learner. I still struggle with concepts taught in first grade.

The next day, I headed to the Iron Bar in between castings. The multilevel venue was under construction. Plastic sheets hung from every doorway. I found Manfred at the upstairs bar, sitting at a makeshift office he'd set up at a Moroccan-tiled coffee table. He looked like a real-life incarnation of a Ken doll, dressed like he was about to play a round of tennis—white shorts, white polo shirt, white cotton knit sweater tied around his shoulders.

"Ronnie says you're a model," Manfred said. "What agency are you with?"

"Nuff Said."

"That bitch wouldn't even call me back. I guess I'm just not what they're looking for anymore," Manfred said. "Have you seen the guys they are using now?"

In the mirror this morning, I thought.

He continued, "They have the bodies of prepubescent girls."

After an uncomfortable pulse, I said, "Yeah."

"Do you work in Milan?"

"I was there for the summer shows."

"Ugh, I'd rather die than march around that industrial shithole. *And* my agent didn't invite me this year. In fact, I haven't heard from that old queen in six months. It's like, sorry I've been at the gym, not shooting up under a bridge. You know what I mean?"

I nodded along. I had never done drugs under a bridge, though I'd been high under one on several occasions.

"But who knows, maybe the pendulum will swing, and they'll start hiring people that actually look like models again," he concluded. "So . . . can you start on Friday?"

During the week, I shot for magazines like *Tiger Beat* that catered to teen girls. On Friday and Saturday nights, I bartended at the Iron Bar. The owner, Rex, looked like a young Dudley Moore but gave off the vibe of Joe Pesci in *Goodfellas*. His boyfriend, Kyle, always greeted me by singing out, "Yes you Canada!"—a slogan from an ad the tourist board of Canada ran in England in the '80s.

Alexander McQueen often came in the early evenings, before the party was raging. Soft-spoken and polite, he introduced himself as Lee and always ordered a double Smirnoff Black and lemonade. McQueen was becoming a huge star in the fashion world—people chased him down the street. I never told him I was a model, but we chatted about clothes. We both dressed in baggy jeans, jumpers, and rugged-looking trainers. Boy George was another regular. He was much stockier than the man I remembered from the "Karma Chameleon" music video. A couple of times, we partied at an after-hours club in Soho. I couldn't help but wonder how a special ed student from Canada ended up hitting the same wrap of coke as Boy George.

Ronnie loved to hear the Iron Bar's "hot goss" while he sipped an afternoon glass of white wine. He'd order his wine and wink at me, saying, "Sometimes you have to treat yourself." One day, I mentioned that the only other straight guy who hung out at the Iron Bar was a coke dealer named Oscar.

"You mean Robodick?"

"I have no idea what you're talking about."

"He's got his dick pierced a million times, doesn't he? Some real Ripley's Believe It or Not shit. Ask 'im. You'll be squinting at the light bouncing off his willie before you know it."

On my next shift, all I had to say was "I heard you have your dick pierced?" and Oscar presented me with Exhibit A. The underside of his penis had so many rings it looked like a pocket-size abacus.

"How many is that?" I asked.

"Twenty-two down the shaft and one through the head. That one's my tribute to Prince Albert."

"Does it work?"

"Course it fucking works, mate," Oscar scoffed, member still in hand. "Birds go mad for it, don't they. Ask her if you don't believe me." With his free hand, he pointed to a woman sitting at the bar. Based on her grinding jaw, she seemed more enamored with Oscar's product.

"I believe you. She's clearly mad for it," I said, walking back behind the bar.

Dozens of club promoters hung out at the Iron Bar. They gave me flyers to parties with names like Bottom Feeders and Glory Hoes. The images on the flyers were even less subtle. Glistening male midsections. The hindquarters of a Ken doll served on a platter. Photos that should be reserved for proctology textbooks.

One afternoon, I forgot to remove the flyers from my pants before I gave Mrs. O'Connor my laundry. The next day, I found them piled neatly beside my clean clothes. After that, she no longer suggested I attend the youth group at her church. She demanded it. I'm sure this incident inspired her to wash my clothes in holy water. I imagined her reminiscing about the good old days when she simply had to hide her pocketbook from Van.

When I told Ronnie that Mrs. O'Connor had found flyers for gay club nights, he became convinced she was trying to seduce me. "She's bang-up gagging for it, mate," he said. "She's going to try and turn you straight."

"But I am straight."

"Those flyers tell a very different story, Phylicia. It's not about carnal pleasures anymore, mate. She's on a mission from God."

Mrs. O'Connor hated my new job. She complained I kept "ungodly hours." My grocery shopping made her inquire, "Is my food not good enough for you?" When I went to the gym, she commented, "Remember, vanity was one of the deadly sins." Attending youth group at her church became a daily conversation. I couldn't avoid her. She was always in the kitchen drinking tea.

One morning, after working at the Iron Bar until 3 a.m., I was awoken by the creak of my bedroom door. Mrs. O'Connor stood at the foot of my bed, frowning. "The sun has been up for hours," she said.

"She's started coming into my room in the morning," I ranted to Ronnie that afternoon as he wrapped bowls of salad with cellophane.

I'd set him up for another seduction joke, but Ronnie just said, "Move in with me then, mate."

"Are you serious?" I didn't even ask where he lived. It didn't matter.

"Just give me a week to prep the flat," he said. "My roomie just left."

That Sunday, Mrs. O'Connor woke me up at 8 a.m. "I think you should accompany me to church," she chided.

I called Ronnie that same afternoon. "Can I move in today?" I asked. "I can't take it anymore."

"Sure, mate."

I ran downstairs and broke the news to Mrs. O'Connor. She threw her hands up and said, "Who doesn't want to live with a friend." You don't, I thought, or you would have turned a blind eye to the fact that I drink bottled water.

I packed my duffel bag and carried it to the front door. There I paused, hearing something I hadn't heard in my entire stay in Clapton. Mrs. O'Connor was laughing.

I found her in the armchair in front of the television. Her little feet dangled high above the floor. She acknowledged me with a nod, still chuckling. I sat down on the couch, curious about the source of her joy. She was watching *Cannonball Run II.*

Together, we watched Dean Martin spy through the peephole of a hotel room. Mrs. O'Connor and I looked at each other and made eye contact while laughing. I'd had sexual encounters that didn't come close to that level of intimacy. It felt like divine intervention.

———————

Ronnie greeted me in front of his place with a bottle of wine in a black plastic bag. "Just made it to the shop before it shut," he said. "I meant to have a kip for twenty minutes, and I slept for three fucking hours. I can't believe it."

"Come on then," he said, opening his wrought-iron gate. I followed him up the stairs. "My gaff is usually in much better shape," he said as he unlocked the door. "I hit Trade last night. It was like jumping into a tank of gay piranhas. Didn't get home till nine a.m., and I bought the lot with me, didn't I?"

Ronnie's long narrow kitchen had a black-and-white tiled floor. A chrome antique display case filled with Disney toys hung on the wall above a dish rack with exactly one plate and one fork. In the living room, the walls were painted a terra-cotta color. A Persian rug lay between two love seats. On the far end of the room stood a wooden loft bed.

"This is incredible," I said.

"Are you taking the piss?"

Before I could answer, Ronnie disappeared into the kitchen. I sat on the love seat facing the fireplace, gawking at a pair of buck horns. Adjacent to the fireplace was another love seat, across from a window. Beside the window was an antique mirror, under which were three Titanic-era trunks. I spotted a framed black-and-white photo and got up for a closer look. Ronnie's father and uncles glared out—flat-nosed and fearsome.

I heard Ronnie pop a bottle of wine and start pouring. "Ah, I fucking love that gorgeous sound," his voice called out. He strutted into the living room and handed me my glass. "Oh, let me grab my fags," he said and flashed back into the kitchen. He emerged with a lit cigarette and sat on the floor, his back against the other love seat.

"Cheers," he said, leaning forward. We clinked glasses. "Welcome home."

I'd always assumed Oshawa would be the only place I would get to call home. I'd had the desire to get out for as long as I could remember but questioned whether I could pull it off. For a person with dyslexia, the world has limits. I had never heard of an illiterate world traveler. I had seen hobos sign their name with an *X*, but they traveled on trains, not planes. I feared I'd be trapped there forever, where nothing ever got better. Now it dawned on me that I could have more than one home. I also thought I'd made all my true friends growing up, but Ronnie was proving that wrong.

Around midnight, Ronnie nodded off with an unlit cigarette in his hand. He woke with a start. "You must think I'm a donut," he said. "I'm going to have night-night fag and get some kip."

When he disappeared into his room, I climbed up into the loft bed. There was no mattress, just plywood and a comforter for padding. I didn't mind at all. I was home.

5

Own It, Mate

I opened my eyes to see Ronnie peering over the edge of the loft bed. "You love a lay-in, don't you?" he said. "I've already been to the market and gotten some really good clobber. Look at this little number." Ronnie held up a vintage Dartmouth sweater. "It's a proper one from the sixties. Single-stitch neck. Look at that lovely bottle-green color."

I sat up, careful not to bump my head on the ceiling. "Can we make coffee?"

"I don't make coffee indoors, I'm afraid. Stinks up the gaff. Smells like a cab dispatcher," Ronnie said and lit a cigarette. "Get dressed, and we'll grab one. My treat."

I climbed down, catching Ronnie's eye in the mirror as he pulled up his sleeves. "Can't cover up the Rolex, can we?" he said, winking.

I went into the bathroom, moving aside a cast-iron Mickey Mouse doorstop. "You piss right loud, though," Ronnie called out.

"You pissed in the middle of the night. I dreamt I was falling over Niagara Falls. After dusk, you're going to have to pee sitting down, I'm afraid. Flat rules."

I laughed, and Ronnie kept riffing. "You rattle the windows, don't you? I'm convinced you bring the stepladder in and piss from the top. I put some clobber that should fit you on my bed, so you don't need to root around in that body bag you brought into my home."

"Thanks," I called.

"I'll meet you downstairs. Don't faff around, though. I know how long it takes you to change out of your funny gym gear after you work out. I fix your five-quid plate when you go into the locker room, and it goes off before you come out."

"What's wrong with my gym clothes?" I asked. But it was too late. I heard Ronnie race down the stairs.

On Ronnie's bed, I found a pair of Evisu jeans and a vintage American football jersey. They fit perfectly. Outside, Ronnie stood in a patch of sunlight, looking up with his eyes closed. He heard the gate close and snapped out of it. "There he is," he said, clapping his hands together, and took off down the street. I followed Ronnie around the corner and saw a row of cafés and restaurants. Suddenly, I recognized my surroundings.

"Holy fuck," I said. "You live a block from Portobello Market."

"'Course I do. You're not in Clapham anymore, mate."

I was too busy jumping up and down to tell him I had lived in Clapton.

"Alrighty," Ronnie said. "Let's take it down a notch, shall we?"

———

My dad called Ronnie the British Kramer. Ronnie had no consistent source of income, yet he was always the first to pick up the tab. Sometimes he'd work the odd shift at the Iron Bar. Sometimes he'd sell clothes from his massive collection at a stall at the Portobello Market. Whatever Ronnie did, he did with pleasure. He once told me he dreamed of playing the saxophone.

"Why don't you learn?" I asked.

"You have to practice two hours a day," he replied. "And the whole time, you can't have a fag."

I'd man the market stall when Ronnie was "gagging for the loo." On my first day, Damon Albarn of Blur walked up. "You doing your stall again, mate?" he asked Ronnie. "I'm going to bring my bird around. You always have the best gear."

Ronnie flashed a smile and said "cheers." It was the same smile and "cheers" he gave a barkeep after he pulled his pint of lager.

"You know the dude from Blur?" I asked when Albarn walked away.

"Just from the neighborhood. Get us a latte then, Phyllis?"

Like everyone I've ever been close to, Ronnie became my proofreader and stenographer. "Ronnie does a great job correcting your spelling," my mom replied to one of our letters. She knew I hadn't suddenly mastered calligraphy and learned how to spell *Portobello*. Not only can I not spell *Portobello*, I can't consistently misspell it the same way. I approach a tough word like *Portobello* calculated and confident, like a boxer. Jab, jab, cross, uppercut.

P-O-R-T. After the *T*, I get the wind knocked out of me and throw uncontrolled haymakers.

"You're winding me up," Ronnie exclaimed when he saw how I spelled *pesto*. "What the fuck is a pissdo? A speedo–adult diaper combo? What a bloke wears in Ibiza if he's incontinent?"

A few weeks after I moved in with Ronnie, I booked several graduation shows for Central Saint Martins, London's prestigious fashion college. At the fittings, I was horrified by the skimpy spandex outfits. I looked like a pale, anorexic aerobics instructor. I thought my booking was an oversight. After years of falling short in school, knowing I didn't have the skills to face the day's challenges, my default mindset was to assume I couldn't possibly be enough. It didn't matter that the designer selected me from thousands of models, then saw me in the clothes and said, "I want him."

After the fitting, I stopped at Selfridges on Oxford Street and bought three tubes of self-tanner. I burst through Ronnie's door, shouting my plan. Ronnie came into the living room armed with a paint roller and a towel. I sat on the towel while Ronnie rubbed fake tanner over my back. I took care of my arms and legs. When I looked in the mirror, beige smear marks covered my body.

"Look at you all smeared and sad," Ronnie said, appearing behind me in the mirror. "You gotta own it, mate," he said. He strutted across the living room in a dress shirt, boxer shorts, and vintage Gucci loafers. "Sell yourself."

What the hell was I thinking, feeling shy or self-conscious? I had worn my mom's bathing suit to a grade twelve party in grade ten. And I'd made out with Lisa Landry.

The next day, in front of my rack of tiny clothes, I thought to myself, You gotta own it, mate. I forced myself to strap on the spandex and step out on the runway. Thankfully, my self-tanner streaks went unnoticed. My last look consisted of bike shorts, a crop top, and a faux fur overcoat.

"When you get to the end of the runway, you must whip off the jacket, then turn and walk back, dragging the coat behind you," the designer instructed, demonstrating the move.

He did it so well, I felt like saying, "Dude, you should do it." When the moment came, I lost my nerve. I simply opened the jacket.

That night, sipping wine with an episode of *EastEnders* playing in the background, I gave Ronnie a play-by-play. I thought he'd be disappointed that I hadn't hit my final pose. Instead, he was proud I'd finished the show.

"I thought you were going to do a runner," Ronnie said. "Your beige-streaked legs were going to start going and not stop till you got back to mine."

Ronnie reminded me of a recent trip to Brighton, where I'd worn corduroy pants on the beach. "We were all celebrating in the sea," he said. "You looked like a geography professor who lost his students."

My alarm blared—3:30 a.m., Sunday morning. I climbed out of my loft bed and got dressed, hearing Ronnie groan awake. We caught a cab to the converted Victorian-era gin distillery that hosted Trade, the hedonistic crown jewel of gay nightlife in London.

"This place is scary," Ronnie said as we gave the bouncer our IDs. "Filled with terrible old queens and horrible Muscle Marys. But some of the people are really quite all right."

Trade's dance floor was packed with topless men gyrating to house music. Between Jubilee Hall and the Iron Bar, I knew a surprising number of people, including the DJ, Fat Tony. Ripped, shirtless men raged with the energy of people who'd just fought to the death. It felt like an after-party for gladiators. They weren't fueled on post-battle adrenaline. Their gusto was manufactured in labs. Drug use was essential for anyone who wanted to socialize at 5 a.m. And most of Trade's denizens had been awake since Friday morning.

When one of Ronnie's mates offered me a pinkish pill, I shook my head. Sometimes I felt like the only one in England not consuming vast amounts of coke and ecstasy. When my fellow models said, "I had a big night," they meant they had partied until dawn. Even photographers and other people I considered adults would flippantly reference these indulgences. Noel Gallagher had famously quipped that in England, "Drugs are like getting up and having a cup of tea in the morning."

I certainly had a couple of cups of tea. But nothing in comparison to the consumption I saw every weekend. I'd changed since high school, when I'd taken LSD every Friday night and doubled the tabs to trip on Saturday. When you take acid, you build up a twenty-four-hour immunity and must double the dosage. I assume it's the universe's way of saying experiences should be reflected on. The same way that after having sex, your genitals need time to regroup. It gives you time to gaze into your lover's eyes. Or barter on the price.

In Oshawa, where drug culture was the only culture, people still stigmatized acid. Even potheads judged us. I certainly judged myself harshly. I felt dirty and worried people talked behind my back. Now I realized I didn't take drugs because I was a bad kid. I was looking for whatever could take me as far from my reality as possible. I needed them to escape the hell of school.

In London, drugs were everywhere, *and* I could indulge without being judged. Offering a Londoner a line of coke guaranteed an evening-long friendship. But I had lost my desire. And my experiences with acid made ecstasy and coke unappealing. Acid takes you somewhere—it's called a trip for a reason. Hard drugs make you feel different about where you are. A paratrooper wouldn't find bungee jumping thrilling. Luckily, I never had a bad trip. It seems my brain thought I had been through enough or couldn't conjure up anything worse than trying to grasp phonics in a public setting.

At 8 a.m., Ronnie and I left Trade and walked to Camden Market. Searching the crowded stalls, Ronnie found a vintage Minnie Mouse toy. At our flat, he Sharpie'd the date and *Phylicia* on Minnie's left foot.

"You're in the archives now, mate," he said.

———

One afternoon, leaving a casting for a trade magazine called *Shoe and Leather News*, I almost walked directly into Andrew. Since our farewell at the Giusti, he had traded his tank tops and motorcycle boots for a suit and overcoat. He'd cut his hair short and coiffed. He looked like a soap opera divorce attorney who bangs his clients.

"Andrew!" I nearly shouted, surprised at how happy I was to see him.

Andrew looked less pleased to see me. "Hey . . . it's Eden, remember?"

"Right. Still hitting the castings hard?"

"Not really. I primarily DJ now."

I imagined the conversation Andrew had with his agent where he declared he wasn't available for a casting unless it was Versace, Karl Lagerfeld, or *Shoe and Leather News*.

"I play mostly house," Andrew continued, looking past me, as if he had read in *Vogue* that being aloof was in this season. "I'm actually in England for a gig."

"A DJ gig in London. Congrats, that's big."

"Well, it's just outside of the city."

"Whereabouts?"

"It's in Beeston. Just outside of Nottingham."

"Cool. Let me give you my number. We should grab a coffee."

Andrew wrote my number on an old Tube ticket. I never heard from him again.

———

One afternoon, I got a call from Victoria, my agent at Nuff Said. "Darling," she said. "You've booked a Fred Perry catalog."

"Really?" I asked.

I took a train to Blackpool, a resort town on the English coast.

In the off season, British seaside towns feel haunted. Blackpool was half-shuttered, as bleak as an abandoned amusement park. On Blackpool's mostly deserted streets, I saw people my age with skin so pale I thought they had applied makeup. Goths in disheveled civilian clothes. What was this zombified look?

At the set, I met Jena, the photographer. She ran a tight ship and had a vision for every photo. At lunch on the first day, she pulled me aside.

"I really like the way the photos are looking," Jena told me. "I was wondering if you'd be interested in shooting an editorial for the *Times* at night."

After the sun went down and the catalog shoot wrapped for the day, Jena and I ran all over Blackpool. She photographed me under streetlamps in Stone Island jackets and space-age trainers. Jena wasn't afraid to head down a sketchy alleyway if she liked the lighting. Her passion was infectious.

Back in London, Victoria lined up more bookings. "I'm getting heaps of requests for you, darling," she told me. A new look called heroin chic was beginning to explode throughout the fashion industry and pop culture. The clothes were inspired by youthful rebellion, grunge music, and indulgence. I felt that I'd come eye to eye with its inspiration when I arrived in Blackpool. Destruction was in. Biceps were out. Designers wanted models with long, stringy hair, pale skin, deep circles underneath their eyes, and emaciated features.

My physique was suddenly in high demand. Designer clothes fit. Instead of being in the wrong place at the wrong time, like being born during the age of literacy, I was right where I needed to be. I wasn't used to strokes of luck. It was as if I had started acing spelling tests because teachers decided to give me marks for originality.

I started walking down runways and shooting editorials for magazines I had heard of, like *GQ*. I shot in the Italian Alps, the British countryside, and the poshest photo studios in London's East End. I landed my first national campaigns for Levi's and a British streetwear company called Firetrap. I immediately got rebooked by Fred Perry. I was cast in a national television commercial for Macleans toothpaste. Every month, I worked with Europe's top designers. And they knew me by my first name.

I didn't grasp it at the time, but modeling was exactly what I needed. I was out of Oshawa. I used to be envious of my friends who'd made it as far as London, Ontario. I was in London, England. All I had to do was arrive on set on time, listen to instructions, and be willing to do what I was told. I didn't have to read reports or reply to emails. Best of all, there were never, ever written instructions.

I did, however, have to succumb to a life of being groped, pushed, undressed, dressed, spun around, and ordered about. A photographer would tell me to dance for him, and then seeing me flail around, quickly shout, "No! No dancing!" Whatever they needed me to be, I had to become. You had to have thick skin, no ego, and a very short memory. Other than manual labor, it was all I felt qualified to do. During an Italian *Vogue* shoot, other male models took their shirts off and lounged around on the floor in between shots, still posing, vying for the photographer's attention, as if they just sat like that naturally. In a group shoot, models schmoozed with the people on set and elbowed their way to a good shot. When a female model was on set, the male models showed off even more.

As a model, I could hide my dyslexia and be viewed as the smart person my parents always said I was. For the first time, I wasn't judged by my grades. But I was also ashamed of modeling and hid the truth about my job from my friends back home. I made Shalom swear never to reveal my secret. That's not so easy when you're posing in countless photo shoots. Sometimes photos from an innocent-appearing set featuring a hot tub get sold to a gay men's magazine, which happens to be the preferred reading material of your friend's gay brother back in Oshawa. That happened. While I figured my friends would tease me for my gay sex appeal, or tease me for being a model at all, all they wanted to know was what it was like to hook up with gorgeous female models. After years of modeling, I was curious what that would be like too.

———

I'd just returned from a shoot for British *GQ* when my high school buddy Alan arrived at my door. Alan was soul-searching through Europe, deciding whether he wanted to marry his high school sweetheart. We drank Oshawa-style, starting at dusk. Around midnight, we got kicked out of a bar called Filthy MacNasty's. We stumbled around north London and hopped a tall fence. I landed awkwardly. Pain raced up my leg. Alan carried me on his back to a hospital, where a doctor told me I had broken my big toe and badly sprained my ankle.

The next afternoon, while I nursed my injuries and my hangover, I got a call from Tino. "Canadese, Mommy has good news for you," he said. "Armani booked you for Fashion Week. No need for a go-see. Now you go model."

Booking Armani without a casting was a triumph, especially since he'd called me "sick chicken." I vowed to impress Armani this time.

A week later, I hobbled along the streets of Milan on a pair of crutches. Passing the Duomo, I thought of my daily Fashion Week pilgrimage. It must have been so off-putting for God to receive prayer requests from a model. He must have said to Himself, "Really? You're a model. Don't you think I've done enough?" But when God realized it was me, He must have admitted that when it came to my physique, He'd kind of phoned it in. I still think it's a huge oversight on God's part that all dyslexics aren't naturally in incredible phys-ical condition. If you can't spell *pectorals*, you should, without a doubt, have them.

At Armani's compound, I limped backstage and found Elena. Her eyes got huge. "What have you done to your being? Can you walk?" she asked.

"What, these?" I replied, lifting my crutches. "I'm accessorizing. Maybe you've heard of it."

Then I saw my first outfit. I had to cram my broken toe into hard-soled dress shoes. I grunted through the pain. At least Arma-ni's clothes fit this time. And my rack was right next to the runway. Twenty other models stood at their racks, counting the number of outfits they had compared to their neighbors. Just before the show, one of Armani's many assistants announced: "Mr. Armani wants to see everyone on the runway for a photo."

I limped the short distance to the runway and stood beside Armani. Then I got hit by a mad rush of half-clad, hemorrhoid cream–scented models. In the photo, which my mom still has, hands reach through the mob to touch Armani. Anything to be closer to a sun-charred legend. In the models' outstretched arms, I see the same desperation captured in photos of refugees reaching for food distributed by UN workers. I'm a floating head in the back row.

I went through hair and makeup and took my place in a long line of models. The last person I saw before I hit the runway was Armani. He adjusted my pants, straightened my belt, made an ever-so-slight adjustment to my sunglasses, and sent me out into the lights.

I hit the illuminated catwalk, trying to control my heart rate and my stride. My stride was an issue. I willed my ankle to function and struck my first pose. When I stepped off the runway, the adrenaline drained away, and searing pain shot up my leg. I hobbled back to my rack. I raced to kick my shoes off and get into the next outfit. One look down, five more to endure.

I must have hidden my limp well. Armani asked me to stay in Milan for a month to model in his showroom. Fashion buyers from all over the world toured Milan's showrooms to choose the clothes they'd stock next season. Models are often sarcastically compared to mannequins. In this situation, we shared the exact same job description. I had worked showroom for Jil Sander—twelve-hour days of sitting around in a cloakroom, waiting for the buyer from a Hungarian department store to decide which pants she wanted to see in action. I was last in the rotation of four models to get the nod and be told to shake my lira maker.

After the show, I went back to my room in a Giusti-style compound and thought it over. I decided to turn down Armani. Cam and some friends from Oshawa were due in London the following weekend. Bailing on them felt like betraying an unspoken Oshawa code to put partying before everything else.

———

When I landed back in England, I picked up a copy of the *Times* of London. In the centerpiece of the Saturday fashion supplement, I saw myself wearing streetwear windbreakers, fitted T-shirts, and baggy pants. The editorial Jena had shot in Blackpool had been published in England's largest newspaper. I felt an unfamiliar emotion. Pride.

Later that day, Cam and three Oshawa boys stumbled through my door, dressed like disheveled executives. My friends from home had gone from Beastie Boys to businessmen overnight after landing their first jobs. They took Ronnie's apartment by storm. "We all drank across the whole Atlantic," Cam announced.

"Take us to a pub," a guy named Dean demanded.

I didn't know Dean very well, but he wasn't a bad guy. I would even put him in the category of "smart-ass," which in the Oshawa hierarchy was almost as high as you could go. The only thing more revered than a smart-ass was a fighter. Smart-asses were celebrated locally, like church potlucks or the opening of new car dealerships. Fighters were renowned throughout the city. If you shitkicked a jock in Beau Valley, the skinheads in south Oshawa would hear about it.

At the Prince Bonaparte, Ronnie manned the bar. "Nice work on the editorial, Phylicia," he said. It felt a far cry from my days of appearing in teen magazines when my only chance of being recognized would be working at the concession stand at a Take That concert.

"You were in the paper?" Cam asked.

"Let's see it," Dean insisted.

"The pictures aren't becoming," I said, embarrassed.

The Oshawa boys chugged beer while I scanned the bar for familiar faces. I didn't want to keep running into English friends bringing up the editorial, and suggested we go around the block to another pub, the Westbourne House. I led the group down Talbot Road, past pastel-colored Victorian architecture.

"What's so fucking great about Europe? Look at this place," Dean slurred, pointing at my favorite powder-blue town house. "There's no driveway. Shit, in Oshawa, I got a two-car garage. There's nowhere to hang a basketball net in this country. I'd rather be dancing at the Red Barn to 'Cotton-Eye Joe.'"

Quite a bold observation for someone who had explored approximately three blocks in the entire continent while blacked out.

At Westbourne House, the music blared and the pub was packed, thankfully not with anyone I knew. I was nervous that Dean would share his opinions on the EU with the other customers. I ordered four Guinnesses, knowing Quinn the bartender pulled a proper pint. She followed Guinness protocol, filling the pint glasses most of the way, letting it settle, then topping them up. I feared the delay might spark a diatribe from Dean about how nothing beats the immediacy of cracking a tall boy of Labatt Blue.

I leaned against the bar and Quinn dropped off the four pints and four complimentary shots of Goldschläger. My old friends formed a semicircle around me. I had never questioned my devotion to the Oshawa boys. Not even when Oshawa-esque shenanigans destroyed my ankle. Now I wondered why I'd turned down Giorgio Armani to drink with a guy who wanted nothing more in life than to hang a basketball net while singing, "Where did you come from? Where did you go?"

Then the door opened, and Jena walked in with a tall guy on her arm. She wore tailored blue coveralls that resembled the uniforms dads in Oshawa wore to work at the GM plant. Jena spotted me, and her eyes lit up. She pushed through the crowd and hugged me.

"This is Oliver," Jena said, introducing her boyfriend.

"Hi, nice to finally meet you. I've heard a ton about you," I shouted over the music.

"You all right, mate?" he asked.

"I said it would be funny if I bumped into you tonight," Jena said, beaming. "Buy you a drink to celebrate?"

"I'll buy you one. G and T?"

Dean peered over Jena's shoulder with Guinness on his upper lip and shouted that he would like one too. I pretended not to hear him. As I caught Quinn's attention, I heard Jena ask, "Did you see Phil's editorial?"

I spun around. Before I could stop him, Cam blurted out, "Phil didn't show me because he said the pictures were unbecoming."

Jena's grin dropped away. I took her by her arm, pulling her close.

"I loved the pictures," I said. "I'm just weird about telling my friends from home about modeling stuff."

"Right," Jena said, avoiding eye contact.

"They found out I was a model when they saw my photos in a gay magazine," I tried to explain.

Jena stared straight ahead.

"They don't understand."

Jena wiggled her arm free. She grabbed Oliver's hand and led him to the other side of the bar. "By the way," she shouted over her shoulder, "I thought you looked great in the photos."

I wished Jena had heard the "Cotton-Eye Joe" conversation. Then she'd understand. I slumped over on the bar. Dean raised his Goldschläger shot. "Shwa boys together forever," he toasted. Cam cheered sheepishly. He knew he'd fucked up.

But it wasn't Cam's fault. Why did I still hide my career? Why had shame followed me across the Atlantic? My shame stemmed from a lifetime of embarrassing moments caused by dyslexia. I was embarrassed that I was the only one who got a zero on the spelling test. Embarrassed that I was constantly being taken out of class and forced to go to the Learning Resource Center. Embarrassed that I needed more time to finish tests. Embarrassed that even with all these allowances, I still ended up in special ed.

Embarrassment is fleeting; it surfaces, then fades. Shame is enduring; it stays with you like a criminal record or the theme of the television show *Muppet Babies*. I knew the world saw special ed students and models very differently. But my learning difference was my portal to both. I'd never been celebrated. Now that the time had finally come, I couldn't accept it. Success was too strange. Like how mustaches were out of style for so long, I'm suspicious now that they're back in. Whenever I'm talking to someone with a mustache who's under sixty-five, part of me feels like I'm on a prank show. I feel like if I take anything they say earnestly, they will rip it off, say "got you," then flick me in the balls.

My brain still talked to me in the same voice as my first-grade teacher's when she said, "Philip can't keep up." I should have been telling myself, "Yeah, dude, you can't read. This is one thing you *can* do. Own it."

I should have taken pride in my work and respected Jena's art. Her passion landed her photos in the *Times* of London while I let my shame override logic, as if I knew more than the fashion editor of a major newspaper. After a lifetime of failing at the hands of my disability, I was to blame for this mistake. And it cost me dearly. I never worked with Jena again. Or Armani.

I scanned the bar. I'd just lit my career on fire and needed a distraction. I spotted a woman with curly blond hair leaning against the counter of the open kitchen.

"What a smoke show," Dean breathed in my ear.

"I'm going to go talk to her," I said.

"Yeah, right."

"Watch me," I said and walked over. The woman looked up and

offered enough of a smile. "I couldn't help noticing you not noticing me," I said.

She chuckled. "Was I being that obvious?" she asked in an inviting Irish accent.

"I'm Phil."

"I'm Alison," she said, tilting her head and smiling.

"Alison . . . I hope I'm saying that right. That is going to be tough to remember. Could you write it down?"

She laughed and reached for a bar napkin.

"And maybe your number too? In case I meet another Alicia."

She handed me the napkin. I made a big show of reading it. "Alison," I corrected myself, staring at her number.

6

Done and Dusted

My female friends tell me that a first kiss is monumental. My first kiss with Alison had everything in their "first kiss tutorial":

1. Atmosphere: walking along the Heath in West Hampstead
2. Spontaneity: leaning in at just the right moment
3. Romance: a slight fog hitting the streetlights

We closed our eyes as our lips connected. I felt like I was floating. Then we walked directly into a parking meter.

I opened my eyes to see Alison's forehead spurting blood. I whipped off my T-shirt, a gift from my Jil Sander showroom days. Alison pressed it against her eye.

"I'll drive you to the hospital," I said, navigating us back to her car.

I let Alison into the passenger side, ran around the back, jumped in the driver's seat, and was stunned by the manual transmission.

"You need to turn the key," Alison said, surprisingly polite. My navy T-shirt had started to glisten with blood.

"I can't drive a stick."

"You're taking the piss."

"Sorry, no one does in Canada. I don't even know if it's legal . . ."

She cut me off. "Fucking switch."

I ran around to the passenger side. Alison climbed into the driver's seat and drove with one hand. "Can you pull the A–Z out of the glove box?" she asked. "I want to make sure I'm going the quickest way."

"Sure."

I flipped through the book of maps, pretending to locate the hospital. Each page swarmed with squiggly roads with impossible-to-read names. I was embarrassed to follow "I can't safely walk down the street or drive stick" with "I can't read," so I said, "looks like we are," and hoped for no further questions.

A doctor closed the gash with three stitches and warned Alison that she might have a concussion. Alison decided I should spend the night to keep an eye on her. When I walked into her ground-level flat, I noticed toys stacked in clear bins. I thought adults collecting toys must be a UK thing, like getting blasted during the day and calling it Sunday roast.

"My friend Ronnie is also a collector," I said.

Alison didn't respond.

The next day, I brought her a bouquet of get-well-soon lilies. She took me by the hand and led me to a white couch in her living room. "I have something I need to tell you," she said.

My mind raced. She had a boyfriend. She had a terminal illness. A boyfriend with a terminal illness.

"I have a daughter," Alison said, as dramatically as if she had delivered the dying boyfriend news. "Her name is Maggie, and she's six. It's complicated because her father is a really famous musician."

I ran through a list of rock stars who struck me as particularly virile. Noel Gallagher? No, Liam. Maybe Ian Brown from Stone Roses, or what's his name . . . the guitar player from the Smiths . . . Johnny Marr. Alison didn't seem like the type who would name her daughter Maggie Marr.

"I wouldn't have cared if you had told me you had a kid," I said. "I love kids."

"I'm sorry I lied. But when I tell guys, they suddenly want to settle down."

Smitten, I bought this line. In retrospect, it was as ridiculous as saying, "I didn't tell you I had been to prison for grand larceny, because I knew you'd make me carry your wallet and phone. I'm so sick of people hearing about my criminal record and insisting that I memorize their pin codes."

Alison warned I wouldn't hear from her for a while. But a few days later, she called and said, "I had something come up." With no further explanation, she dropped Maggie off at Ronnie's place. Maggie looked like a young Drew Barrymore. Her sobriety and reasonable eyebrows chipped away at my Gallagher brother theory.

We soon exhausted every child's favorite activity of staring at Ronnie's cashmere sweater collection. After doing the same with his Disney toys, Maggie and I set out for a café on the other side of

Portobello Market. The Sunday market heaved with people, and I gripped Maggie's hand. In the middle of the chaos, I heard her little voice say, "My legs stopped working."

I felt a sudden sensation of dead weight. Maggie had collapsed. Even her hand went limp. She repeated, "My legs stopped working." My agitation became laughter. I stood in the middle of people who were darting from stall to stall, laughing hysterically.

"Maggie, please stand up," I said, trying and failing to sound serious.

Maggie realized she was killing and got limper.

"My legs stopped working" became our first inside joke. Maggie was also a remarkable mimic. She sagged her pants and imitated my Canadian accent, saying, "Hey Al, hey Mag, I'm going OUT." And she dabbled in observational humor. "You always claim to be 'running around,'" she observed. "Yet I've never actually seen you run."

To this day, I claim to be constantly running around, although I rarely move fast. It's my mind that's racing. Disorganization is a clinical symptom of dyslexia. Even when my body is still, my thoughts jump from things I must remember to things I've forgotten. I only learned about this symptom a few years ago and finally understood why I feel perpetually overwhelmed.

Alison tried to use my dyslexia as a teachable moment. "Phil has struggled to read and write his whole life," she explained to Maggie. "It's a challenge he faces every day."

"I can read to him," Maggie said.

From then on, Maggie read to me from her Harry Potter books.

But when I asked her to pick up her stuff before her mom came home, she whispered, "At least I can read," just loud enough for me to hear.

Soon I was head over heels for both of them. With my mom on the other side of the world, I relied on Alison for simple tasks I couldn't do on my own. She let me dictate the addresses of my go-sees and booked all my travel. When I booked trips, I often input the wrong dates. She helped me pack for shoots the night before, when she saw the amount of stress caused by getting out the door in the morning. My life functioned more smoothly with Alison running it.

"I'm going to move in with her," I told Ronnie at a café where we had stopped for a prework coffee. Although at the last minute, he'd decided to get a glass of white wine.

"Are you sure, mate?"

"I'm there all the time anyways."

"It's easy to move in. But tough to move out," he warned and swallowed the last of his wine. "If it doesn't work out, can you imagine leaving Mary?"

"Maggie," I corrected him.

"Are you sure? Why did you let me order that? I'm pissed, aren't I?" he asked. "Now I need to go home and have a kip."

———

After I moved in, Alison became very open about the fact that she hated that I was a model. She was convinced I'd cheat on her with all my coworkers. I pointed out that female models tended to date actors, footballers, and musicians. Not unlike Alison, who continued to keep the identity of Maggie's father under wraps.

This mystery man even intrigued my old friend Pugs, whose default was to shrug his shoulders when it came to other people's business. He'd phone me from Toronto and guess a random musician from across the pond. I'd pick up the receiver and hear, "Echo and the Bunnymen." When Alison finally revealed his identity, I learned he was an Irish musician revered by those in the know. But I had never heard of him.

One day, Alison picked me up from a photo shoot and overheard the female stylist compliment my T-shirt. The next time I went to wear it, I discovered Alison had bleached a hole in the center. Once, I couldn't go with her and Maggie on a trip to Mykonos because I booked a last-minute shoot. On the day of the gig, Alison called me from a pay phone, whispering into the receiver, "There's a man following me. We're in danger." Then she hung up.

My mind raced with images of the woman I loved being accosted by a DJ version of Hercules. I obsessed about Alison's and Maggie's safety all day. I didn't impress anyone I was shooting with, including the client. When the shoot wrapped, Alison called back and acted like nothing was wrong. She only vaguely remembered the stalker.

One Sunday morning, Alison drove me to the gym as I ate muesli out of a thick ceramic bowl. Considering muesli a suitable on-the-go meal proves my brain is wired differently.

"I don't understand why you need to go to the gym so much,

why it's more important than spending time with me and Maggie," Alison said.

"It's not more important," I replied. Working out was always a point of contention. Trying to better myself meant I wanted to meet someone else.

Alison pulled over under the Ladbroke Grove underpass. "There are women there. I see how they look at you."

"So now me working out is an issue? You know inmates are permitted to do it, right?"

"It's suspicious how you just *need* to do it."

I threw the empty bowl onto the car floor. It broke in half.

"Very mature," Alison said. "And don't slam my fucking door."

Alison and Maggie picked me up later that night from Ronnie's. In the car, I noticed the broken bowl.

"Why did you leave it there?" I asked Alison after Maggie had gone to bed.

"Maggie should know what happened to our bowl," Alison replied.

I've only heard my parents have one argument, and they recently celebrated their fiftieth anniversary. I don't have the temperament to try to beat their record, but I do think that children should be spared the ugliness of hearing adults go at it. The same way I think it's for the best that children aren't privy to their sports heroes' postgame exploits. There's no upside to a nine-year-old hearing that Tiger Woods was insatiable when it came to prostitutes.

But I couldn't leave Alison. I needed her vital support. I sacrificed tranquility for the sake of a live-in proofreader and life organizer. My reliance on partners has stopped me from leaving many toxic relationships. There's a long list of people who have taken care of me in ways I couldn't take care of myself. I've learned this pattern is typical of people who share my learning difference. Dyslexia affects so much more of our lives than just being unable to read subtitles. I'd kill for it just to mean I have to bullshit my way through conversations about French cinema.

Alison pushed me to try anything other than modeling. She suggested I study music. I love music, but learning to read it seemed impossible. Reading words was still very much a work in progress. I was conflicted. Work was better than ever. I had finally broken into lucrative advertising campaigns and even started booking more television commercials. I was saving money for the first time in my life. And I got to treat Maggie, picking her up from school on my lowrider bicycle, putting her on the crossbar, and heading to our favorite bakery. But after years of meeting photographers and designers, people with true passion and vision, I realized I wanted that too. I just had no clue what "that" was.

I had a hint, though, one Thursday afternoon when I got a call from Victoria. "Darling, how long would it take for you to get to Soho?" she asked. "I got a casting for you and it pays a packet."

I happened to be with Ronnie in Soho at Bar Italia. Even though Ronnie felt, "This place is kind of naff now."

Victoria told me the address. I repeated it in my head. Trying to spell it would only confuse things. I rushed through the streets.

The audition was for an American car commercial. As soon as I arrived, they brought me in. It clearly had been a long day and they were ready to pack it in. I had to improvise driving along in the British countryside, ho hum, when all of a sudden, the road turned into a roller-coaster track. When the casting agent raised her hand to signify the change, I really let loose. My reaction made everyone in the room laugh. I loved the process, and the directors loved me. I wondered if there might be something to this improv thing.

The next week I traveled to Swindon on the train. For the next three days, I shot on a small country road surrounded by rolling hills. The ad had a big budget. We were served gourmet meals in a converted double-decker bus. One lunch break, I joined the creative team. They were from New York. The youngest member of the team was slightly older than me and hung out at some of my favorite New York bars, like Max Fish and the Cherry Tavern.

"I'd give anything to be back in New York," I said between bites of shepherd's pie.

"Give everything. Work your ass off and you'll be there."

I was unsure exactly what I should work my ass off at.

I decided to enroll in a local improv class. We met in a damp church basement. My fellow wannabe improvisers were a retired kindergarten teacher, a middle-aged man who appeared unhoused and referred to himself as a young entrepreneur, a teenager who fit the profile of a school shooter, and a guy in lederhosen. In the first five minutes of class, Mr. Lederhosen made three attempts to perform what he called a "traditional Italian dance number."

It's extremely hard to make it in comedy, yet the barrier to entry is nonexistent. You don't even need to spell your name right on the sign-up form at an open mic. Any series of letters on the page will get you onstage. Once you're onstage, even if it's a milk crate, you're a comedian. Every other performing art has qualifications. You can't just throw on a Viking helmet, start busting out figaros, and be considered an opera singer.

My first scene took place in a supermarket. My improv partner said something ludicrous about the groceries. "The cantaloupes are coming to life, they are chasing us," I said, reacting honestly. "And the acid is kicking in."

My line got a big pop. When I heard that laughter, I flashed back to being sixteen years old in Tommy and Steve Love's basement in Oshawa, where the acid was also kicking in. Their parents were never around, so we had free rein to drink, smoke hash off red-hot butter knives, prank call local businesses, and bust each other's balls. I always had the fastest comeback, the quickest jab. "King Jock" Zack O'Neill didn't care for the way I held court. He interrupted my jokes to ask, "How much can you bench?"

"I coach Little League," I replied. "I benched the whole team."

My friends still referenced that joke. In the classroom, I was always the slowest learner. In sports, I was the skinniest kid with the least skills. Dyslexia affects hand-eye coordination and depth perception, two things needed in any athletic endeavor. In that basement, I was the master of ceremonies. It was my gift. But because it couldn't be quantified on a report card or a scoreboard, it went unacknowledged. By me, at least.

That night in England, in a basement of prayer, not of hot

knives, I realized making strangers laugh felt good. I couldn't believe how good. As good as making my friends and family laugh. I recalled a conversation with my Canadian friend Anna, who'd recently visited London. Originally from Vancouver, she had told me about her city's vibrant improv theater scene. "I have a friend who just got involved," she told me.

"That would be a dream," I replied.

Anna gave me a strange look. "I just watched you in a fashion show for agnès b."

———

Alison kept changing the spelling of her name, going with a *y* instead of an *i*, and sometimes using two *l*'s, which is just a messed-up thing to do when your boyfriend is dyslexic. Ultimately, she changed her name entirely to Sloane. Then Alison-Alyson-Sloane returned from a trip home to Ireland with herpes. Yes, herpes.

Alison swore she hadn't cheated. She claimed she must have contracted the virus long before we got together and that it had been lying dormant. Yet I'd noticed she groomed herself extensively down there before her trip to Ireland. I went into detective mode, looking for clues in the UK's socialized health-care system. I called the nurse hotline several times a day. I quickly became an expert on herpes.

On a late-night call, a male nurse gave me the straight dope. "Sweetheart," he said, "she came home bald as a cue ball with blisters. Let's be real: the girl cheated on you. Although herpes are a dime a dozen, you don't want them. Especially from someone you shouldn't be with in the first place. Run for the hills."

I hung up and thought: Run for the hills? I'm sprinting for the mountains.

I packed two years' worth of stuff and put it in Ronnie's "little room," a giant walk-in closet he used for storage. The next morning, Ronnie made me a Milky Dilky, simmering instant coffee and milk in a saucepan.

"Never make these if I'm not home," he said. "You'll burn down the gaff. I hate to say it, Phylicia, but I told you so. It's the jealous ones you got to watch out for. They don't trust you because you can't trust them."

"You were right."

"She used that lil Mary to lure you in. I didn't trust that little one either. I know she touched my cashmere when no one was clocking her and rubbed her little leprechaun face on them. I found little boogies in my mauve section and all."

That night, I flew to Düsseldorf, Germany, to shoot a winter-wear catalog. The gig paid me the most money I'd ever earned modeling. Another male model named Jason Drydon and I tried on four hundred winter coats. Jason looked so much like a young Paul Newman that it was distracting. We had crossed paths before in Milan. I liked him but couldn't relate to his all-in attitude when it came to modeling. He planned to ride those cheekbones till the wheels fell off. After the last day of shooting, the photographer and I walked down by the Rhine River.

"I don't want to shoot parkas all my life," he told me. "But it's a stop on the way to the top."

I never thought about modeling in those terms. When I was

in a bad place, I thought it would last until I died. I think that's because school had been such a long, painful haul that never let up, like a choke hold by a UFC fighter who refuses to recognize a tap-out.

That night at 2 a.m., Alison called my hotel room. She claimed she was calling to say hi, but I knew she wanted to check if I was alone.

"The shoot was an all-male crew," I snapped. "And aren't you the one who cheated on me?"

"I told you, it was dormant!"

"I'm moving to Vancouver," I said. "I'm really going to fucking miss Maggie."

Before she could respond, I slammed down the phone and yanked the cord out of the wall.

My relationship was "done and dusted," as Ronnie would say. So was my modeling career. Even a handsome payday, which technically all model jobs are, didn't mean much if I wasn't doing what I loved. I didn't want to make the mistake that people often make in movies about bank robberies and have one last job backfire. Instead of going to jail, I'd land a ten-year stint in a showroom for a designer who featured only black-and-white striped clothing. Between the car commercial and winter coat extravaganza, I had enough money to start over.

I flew from Düsseldorf to London to pack up my life. It was going to be hectic. Organizing stuff in suitcases was almost as hard as organizing letters into words. I landed at Heathrow and headed to Ronnie's. He poured me a glass of wine for my nerves. And one for himself because it would be rude otherwise.

"You faff around for ages packing," Ronnie said. "Thought I'd make it easier." He pointed at one of his Titanic-era trunks. "Cleaned it out for you too. If I didn't, you'd never make your flight."

I gave Ronnie the tightest hug I had ever given anyone.

"Easy, Phylicia. Let's take it down a notch, shall we, mate?" Ronnie said. "And don't ruin the trunk with a Grateful Dead sticker."

I had a surprise for Ronnie too. I handed him an envelope. He took out a silver necklace he had coveted for years. I'd had *nothing but love* engraved on the back. Ronnie wasn't a sentimental dude. I once caught him reselling a birthday gift at the market while there was still cake left. But projectile tears shot out of his ducts.

"I love you, mate."

"I love you too."

I said goodbye to Ronnie, to London, to Europe, and to modeling. It was time to go home.

7

Mind on the Moon

In the spare bedroom of my parents' condo, my mom helped unpack Ronnie's trunk. My parents had sold their house in Oshawa and relocated to Vancouver, ending my connection to my childhood home. Unmoored in a new city, my mom had sought out a place that felt like home. She started volunteering at a school, helping kids learn to read. I helped her fold my clothes, organizing them into tidy stacks in the closet. She didn't press when I told her my career as a fashion model was over. She told me to take as much time as I needed to figure out my next steps.

My bedroom was located downstairs from the kitchen and living room, where the curtains were always shut against the fifth-floor view because of my dad's fear of heights. Although my mom was steadily inching them open with the patience of a Tibetan monk, or what a Tibetan monk would describe as the patience of Joan Hanley.

I'd been home for a week when I was woken by the phone. The

condo was concrete and quite soundproof, so for me to hear the living room phone ringing all the way down in my room, it must have been happening for a while. When I got to the top of the stairs, I read the clock on the stove. It was 6 a.m., and after doing some quick transatlantic math, I knew who was calling.

"Phil, my sister's cancer came back," Alison said before I could get out a hello.

"I'm so sorry," I said, my throat still thick with sleep. "Fuck, I'm so sorry."

"Are you really? Are you sorry enough to actually help me? I'm going to have to go to Dublin to take care of her. I need you back in England, Phil."

"I'm not sure that's a good idea," I said.

"Maggie needs you. If you don't come back, she will have to go live with her dad."

Alison was hitting me where it hurt. Whenever Maggie's dad took her for the odd weekend, she returned looking like she'd contracted meningitis.

"What are you doing in Canada that's so important that you can't come and save a child?" Alison asked.

I couldn't give her a good answer. "I'll come back," I relented. "For Maggie."

I flopped on my parents' couch, trying to convince myself this was a good idea. I hated that the Atlantic Ocean was no match for Alison's mind games. But I despised the idea of Maggie not being cared for properly. For almost two years, I'd picked Maggie up from school, made her breakfast, and taken her to doctors' appointments. I acted as her guardian in every way except for helping with her spelling homework. Back with my parents, I'd regressed to feeling like a child myself.

My mom shuffled into the kitchen in her bathrobe. "Oh dear, I didn't expect you to be up. How about some French toast?"

"I've got to go back to England."

"What do you mean, dear?"

"Alison's sister's cancer came back. I need to go take care of Maggie or her dad will have to . . ."

"What are you doing?" my mom shouted. "She's manipulating you!"

I had never seen Joan Hanley lose her cool. She never lost it when, as a kid, I threw my homework across the room. She never lost it when I came home drunk or stoned as a teenager. Or when I totaled her car two weeks after getting my license. She'd just said, "I'm happy you're okay."

"She's taking advantage of you, dear," my mom said, slamming her hand on the dining room table. "I'm sorry her sister is sick. But we both know Alison wouldn't let Maggie live with that man. If nothing else, she's a good mom."

The thing is, I hadn't realized that Alison-level manipulation was even possible. I'd had such easy relationships with my mom, my sister, and my high school girlfriend that I figured every relationship I had with a woman would be just as easy and pleasant. It's like I had grown up with house cats and then I went to pet a lion, and it ate my arm and almost gave me herpes. Whatever my next step was, it would not involve going back to England.

But I had no inkling as to what that next step would be. Modeling had brought me to Europe. But it wasn't a solution to living with dyslexia. Sure, it wasn't an office job. I didn't have to read or write emails. I didn't have to pore over corporate documents. My agents handled all my paperwork. But modeling wasn't a transferable skill. I couldn't go into a job interview and say, "I think what this company needs is a guy who looks decent in an oversize blazer under the right lighting."

You think you've had a quarter-life crisis? Try doing that with barely a high school education, the reading level of a first grader, and a broken heart.

To say I was directionless implies there was the intention of movement. I spent my time flicking through television channels. One night, I stopped on a new show called *Temptation Island*. Couples arrived on an island inhabited by beautiful and amorous singles who tempted them to be unfaithful. The show starred no other than Eden (née Andrew), who tasted the forbidden fruit of his namesake and cheated on his long-term girlfriend on national television. He was no longer "primarily a DJ"; he was an internationally televised manwhore.

My mom urged that I should really get some fresh air. One afternoon, I walked downtown and bought a ticket to *Man on the Moon*, a biopic about Andy Kaufman. Jim Carrey, as Kaufman, appeared on screen wearing a goofy suit, his eyes darting left to right. I was transfixed when Kaufman visited a Transcendental Meditation retreat in Hollywood. Sitting cross-legged in front of a bead-wearing guru holding a bouquet of flowers, Kaufman opened his eyes and raised his hand.

"I would like to thank you, your holiness," he said. "My heart is radiating pure energy. I would like to ask you a question. Is there a secret to being funny?"

"Yes," the guru replied. "Silence."

Meditation had been on my mind since high school, when I'd learned my favorite dyslexic, Bob Weir, was a practitioner. A yogi had given him a mantra that he used every day. Oshawa had no meditation centers, so I continued to use psychedelics to get closer to Bob.

And on my first visit to New York, Shalom introduced me to supermodel Amber Valletta, who'd just returned from a yoga and meditation retreat. While we sipped wine in Shalom's apartment, Valletta made an oral sex joke inspired by her husband's newly sprouted beard.

"How did you feel after?" I asked.

"After he went down on me?"

"No, the meditation," I told the most beautiful woman I had ever met. I was thinking, Enough about your vagina already! Tell me about the tranquil sensation of the empty mind.

In England, I'd even taken a Reiki workshop. Unfortunately, the only overlap between Reiki and meditation was the attendees' love of patchouli oil. My level-one Reiki certificate is the closest thing I have to a college diploma, but I didn't learn to meditate.

Now, I had a name: Transcendental Meditation. I scribbled my interpretation of the words on a scrap of paper I always kept in my pocket. When the credits rolled, I hustled home. I rushed into the kitchen, where my mom was preparing dinner, and retrieved the phone book from a drawer. I recited the alphabet in my head, trying to locate *T*.

"Let me help you, dear," my mom said. "Which word are you looking for?"

"Transcendental Meditation."

Her index finger magically appeared on the entry for the Transcendental Meditation Centre of Vancouver.

With my mom's help, I researched TM. The yogi from *Man on the Moon* was inspired by Maharishi Mahesh Yogi, who'd famously taught the Beatles to meditate after they'd made *Sgt. Pepper*. And he'd been Bob Weir's teacher. Weir's dyslexia was so severe that sometimes when he looked at trees on a hillside, they shifted from one place to another. But TM had helped him. And I hoped it would help another dyslexic find serenity in a world set up without him in mind.

———

I arrived at the Transcendental Meditation Centre of Vancouver on a Tuesday night. I was taken aback by the Courtyard by Marriott vibes. Surely, my instructor would stand out like a sore thumb. I expected a half-hippie professor, half-zenned-out mentor who'd help me glimpse another dimension that would pull me helplessly into a flowing current.

Instead I met Stewart. This guy was no Maharishi. Stewart looked like he had passionate opinions on printers. As we shook hands, I realized he would be my guide on this celestial journey, sweater vest and all.

Stewart ushered me into a conference room that seemed like a place where insurance brokers compared annual sales numbers. On the wall above a long table, I spotted a portrait of Maharishi. I recognized him by his peaceful smile and long flowing hair. Some students had already arrived. We all were determined to find something, like a drunk woman with one shoe. I sat next to a guy in his fifties who looked like he used to party with Bob Seger.

"I'm Dale. Used to do TM back in the seventies when it first hit North America," he said. "Did it every day. We did *everything* every day back then. I'm here for a refresher."

Refresher? I never thought of enlightenment as something that wore off, like the novelty of a pet snake. I looked around the room at my fellow seekers. There was a bike enthusiast, one of those pariahs who socialize in head-to-toe spandex. If Vancouver had a mascot, it would be a reusable water bottle in aerodynamic garb. Besides Trance Armstrong, I saw a couple who looked and smelled like they made their own nut butter and a young executive in a sport coat. The executive filled me with unholy judgment. Using a sacred practice to give you a capitalist edge? Despicable. Never mind that I had prayed at the Duomo for lucrative modeling bookings.

After the last would-be meditator sat down, Stewart addressed the class. "I want to welcome you to Transcendental Meditation. Or TM as it's often called. The process is simple. Not because it's meditation for beginners but because the method has an elegant simplicity."

I thought, Stewey baby, would it kill you to throw on a string of beads?

Stewart hit Play on a DVD player. I prepared to roll my eyes. For years, I'd sat in a classroom without the faintest idea of what anyone was talking about. When I couldn't grasp a concept, I made fun of it. But today's learning materials were visual—testimonials of every-day people recounting TM's impact. The videos riveted me. I watched Maharishi, wrapped in a blanket, walk beside Lake Louise in Alberta. He compared the conscious mind to the choppy surface of the water. With our individual mantra, he said, we could go beneath the con-scious mind to the subconscious, the calm water beneath the surface.

Stewart assured us anyone could do TM. I didn't question my ability, which was audacious for someone with my track record in a classroom. Over the next four nights, I sat in the front row of Stewart's classroom, focused and attentive. I learned that Transcen-dental Meditation doesn't attempt to control the mind. It lets it flow freely with the simple guidance of the mantra. You didn't need to pay attention to unwanted thoughts. You could accept them and calmly go back to your mantra. That idea stopped me in my tracks. A lot of unhelpful thoughts crossed my mind, like, I can't spell *transcendental,* or that I might not have my own place for a long time because my parents are really healthy.

By the end of the week, our fifteen-person class had dwindled to eight. The human water bottle had cycled away. Mr. and Mrs. Nut Butter were still in the house, as was the young executive. I had judged him too harshly. He reminded me of my beloved Pugs, business slacks and all. At the end of our final class, Dale pointed a nicotine-stained finger at my Grateful Dead shirt.

"I saw the Dead in Vancouver at the Pacific Coliseum in like 1976," he said.

"They played the Pacific Coliseum for the last time in 1974," I corrected him. "Whoa, I can't believe you were at the show. That 'Eyes of the World' is incredible."

Dale looked at me like I had been tracking him all this time.

On Saturday, I returned to the Centre for my first meditation experience. Stewart had instructed me to bring pieces of fruit and flowers as an offering. He led me into a room just big enough for two chairs. Candles burned at the base of a shrine decorated with flowers, incense, and a picture of Maharishi's teacher, Guru Dev. This was more like it. Even Stewart seemed imbued with cosmic energy, though he still looked like a white Urkel.

I gave Stewart his fruit and flowers. He placed them on a brass tray beneath the shrine. And then he gave me something that I carry to this day: my mantra. I've never told anyone what it is.

"Close your eyes and take some deep breaths," Stewart instructed. He introduced my mantra to the practice and told me to "Repeat it with me with gentle effortlessness." I said my mantra aloud. Stewart and I repeated it together ten times. Then he told me to repeat it silently.

I went deep. I was completely aware of my surroundings and simultaneously transported somewhere else. Time dissipated. I experienced a subtle but undeniable pleasure. It felt . . . transcendental. When Stewart rang a gentle chime, I felt as though I'd experienced a dream while fully awake. The kind that stays with you all day. The kind that changes how you see the world. I was all in.

"When can I meditate again?" I asked.

"This evening before dinner."

I walked out of that room a changed man. Heroin users reminisce about their first shot of dope. I'll always be chasing the high I had that night at the Vancouver TM Centre.

From that moment forward, I meditated twice a day, once in the morning and once in the evening, for twenty minutes. I started to see the world more clearly. Positive thoughts came easier. Negative ones didn't stick around as long. My anxiety lifted. I stopped obsessing over details. I realized I had spent my life exhausting myself over school, pointlessly obsessing for hours over pages of text. I had needlessly beaten myself up. I should have celebrated myself and everything I had accomplished. I started to appreciate myself, for the first time, for who I was.

I know what you're thinking: So what? Everyone's meditating these days. We're all mindful and thoughtful and diving into our inner peace. But this was way before mindfulness was a thing. Way before apps guided us through meditation sessions during our train rides to work. Way before any of this was accepted by the masses. Fuck, yoga was fringe. Don't forget, I found the number in the phone book.

My mom remarked on my improvement. "You seem more aware of others, dear," she told me. My dad, on the other hand, found the idea unsettling. I overheard him tell one of my friends, "He'll have to call you back, he's meditating," with the same disapproving tone as if I were polishing my Fabergé egg collection.

During my evening sessions, I often had painful thoughts of Alison. I tried to accept them. They were the chop on the surface of the water. Once I let them pass, they stopped reappearing. Thoughts of Maggie, even happy ones, still conjured tears. But smiles too.

When my mind flowed freely, my thoughts kept returning to that night in the church basement in England. The first night I'd made a group of strangers laugh. I thought about how good I'd felt. I wanted that feeling again. I took the Aquabus across the water to Granville Island and signed up for TheatreSports 101. I had walked down runways in front of the fashion industry's most important and judgmental figures. What could a crowd of anonymous Van-couverites possibly do to me?

TheatreSports 101 met in the theater where the shows took place. The teacher, a serious, thin man in an oversize plaid shirt, told us to form a circle on the stage. I stood next to a big, square-shaped guy who was at least six foot three. His thick brown hair jutted straight out from his head. He introduced himself as Nathan.

The teacher held up a finger for silence and said we'd begin with an "energizer" exercise called Zip, Zap, Zop. My classmates fired sounds around the circle, each word sending the game in a differ-ent direction. My brain struggled to process the unfamiliar words.

"Zoup," I guessed when someone pointed my way.

"Zop," the teacher corrected.

The game swung around the group, landing back on me. Again, I Zouped. I was killing with my classmates. The teacher waved his arms and made us start over. By my third Zoup, Nathan's broad frame doubled over with laughter. Making someone laugh like that is an intimate thing. Often when people talk about their favorite dramatic actors, they say they like them. But when they discuss Robin Williams, they use the word *love*.

"Embrace these dumb games," Nathan told me.

"Right," I said.

"I'm serious, they help."

I had always been guarded. Played it cool. When you can't read, you have to put on a brave face. In school, I adopted a first-day-in-prison mentality. Never cried when teachers tried to teach by humiliating me. There's a photo of me at seven, standing beside Santa with my hands in my pockets. Even at that age, I thought sitting on his knee wasn't a good look.

A few classes later, our teacher instructed the class to line up at the side of the stage. One by one, the students faced him, and he shouted a prompt, trying to throw them off. When they hesitated, they got in their own way.

"You are standing on a desert island," the teacher called when it was my turn.

I walked to the edge of the stage and placed a hand above my eye line, staring at an imaginary horizon.

"What do you see?"

"Shelley Long."

The line got a huge laugh from the class. I hadn't seen or consciously thought of the *Cheers* star in many years. But she was right there when I needed her. A lesson in trusting my subconscious.

"You're getting faster," Nathan told me on the Aquabus after class.

Nathan and I walked from my parents' condo under the Burrard Street Bridge to a patch of grass beside the seawall. We rehearsed with the ocean and mountains as our backdrop. When the weather wasn't nice, we did it at my parents' squash court. Nathan read me his additions to a sketch we'd cowritten. Our writing system worked around my dyslexia. I added quick lines and broad strokes; Nathan took care of formatting the words on the page. That night, we ran the scene until dark. Two adult men making each other laugh in a park with no audience is teetering on madness. But Nathan and I were fully immersing ourselves and seeing results.

Nathan studied comedy the way I obsessed over the Grateful Dead. He'd taped every episode of *Saturday Night Live* since he was five—not unlike Deadheads making bootlegs of shows. He knew every line from every *Kids in the Hall* and *SCTV* sketch. He'd say, "Bob Odenkirk's inspiration for *Mr. Show* came from *Monty Python*" like it was common knowledge. He once reminded me it was Don Knotts's birthday.

"Comedy is a craft," Nathan told me. "A skill you can hone."

I started setting a morning alarm. I sat at the kitchen table with my mom and practiced improv writing games. I'd ask my mom for a prompt and she'd say, "Oh, I don't know, dear. A communist tea party?" and I'd slowly draw letters to form a scene. Writing even a few words was exhausting. I took a less-is-more approach. I didn't need extra words. Just enough to make my mom laugh.

And every day I meditated. Twenty minutes. Twice a day. After my second meditation session, I solved problems in my sketches. Both improv and meditation utilize the subconscious. Meditation leads to subtle developments that come to fruition over time. Improv requires quick flashes, like a match striking the pack. Bob Weir says that when he's playing music, time goes away. I, too, experienced time dissipating while performing. It felt like the opposite of school, where time was heavy and dull.

Nathan and I went from performing in a park to being asked to participate in a long-running improv night at a bar over the bridge from my parents' condo. We went back and forth with rewrites on our sketch like woodworkers building a table. Nathan assembled a structure; I sanded out the rough edges. The longer we worked, the sturdier we made the sketch. So this was what progress felt like? So this was what everyone else had been feeling all this time?

———

Early one morning, my parents' phone rang. My friend Anna McRoberts was on the other line. Anna had gone to Queen's University, two hours east of Oshawa, with Pugs and most of my high school crew. She'd become an executive at Keystone Entertainment. You know those talking dog movies kids love? She makes those. You should see her house.

"I'm on set in Jamaica and we just added a scene to the movie," Anna said. "Could you write a few lines of funny dialogue?"

"Seriously? Why me?"

"Phil, you're the funniest person I know."

"Thank you. That means a lot, but . . ."

Anna didn't let me finish. "So the movie's about a chimpanzee detective and in the scene he's walking on the beach in a tuxedo."

"Wait, are you sure you want me?"

"You've always been funny. Remember the party where you directed a Christmas play and cast Pugs as baby Jesus without him knowing?"

"You nailed Joseph, by the way. When do you need it?" I asked.

"We're shooting it right after lunch. So . . . an hour? Just give me three lines of dialogue and a few alts."

"Okay," I said, though I had no idea what "alts" were.

When I hung up, my core temperature rose. I had to write chimp dialogue at the drop of a monkey-size Sherlock Holmes hat.

I closed my bedroom door and put on a Grateful Dead show. I didn't think. I wrote. And the words tumbled out of, I assume, my subconscious. By the third song of the first set, I had three lines and a bunch of alts, which I guessed were extra lines of dialogue. Anna's assistant chuckled as I dictated my jokes over the phone.

"Phil, this is great stuff," Anna said when she called after they wrapped for the day. "Even the chimp trainer laughed. And she's miserable."

Soon I was working on short scenes for Anna's company. I got the call when the other writers were stumped. Anna's assistant would drop off scripts with gaping holes where they needed a scene. Attached to the scripts were notes like: *Chimp finds fingerprints on the bank vault.* That meant they needed a set piece, a long scene of physical comedy, like in *Home Alone* when Macaulay Culkin sets booby traps for the Wet Bandits. Rule of thumb: havoc must ensue.

I'd work all night, scrawling block letters on a yellow legal pad. My brain was really good at imagining a blank canvas and filling it in with hijinks—maybe even *because* I was dyslexic. I remembered reading about a famous dyslexic architect who could do the same type of thing—he could stand on a flat site before anything was built and picture the whole building. When I was happy with a scene, I'd tear out the page and tuck it into the script. The next morning, an assistant would pick up the script with yellow paper sticking out everywhere. When her car left the driveway, I'd pass out, exhausted.

Ultimately, these patchwork gigs led Anna to ask me to come in and meet her boss, Robert Vince. At Keystone headquarters, Vince sat with his feet up on his desk and his hands behind his head, a posture I thought only appeared in movies. On the wall behind him hung a giant *Air Bud* poster, depicting a golden retriever dunking a basketball.

"I got an idea," Vince said, leaning back in his chair. "Air Bud has puppies."

"A lot of sequel potential," I said.

"Exactly. First things first. We need names."

Each of the five puppies had a distinct personality. The names had to fit them perfectly, and each name needed to involve the word *bud*. I came up with a dozen options, and Keystone chose Mudbud, B-dawg, Buddha, Budderball, and Rosebud—the last being named after one of Jerry Garcia's guitars.

For *Air Buddies*, Anna would drop off scripts with some formatting in place but leave huge gaps. Sometimes the description would be clear: *We meet the buddies.* Other times rather vague: *vineyard/ chaos.* Drafts were due every three weeks. Suddenly I was doing what I'd hoped to avoid until I died: reading and writing. For ten hours a day, I struggled through simple lines of dialogue. When exhaustion set in, I added an extra twenty-minute meditation session. Meditation couldn't cure my dyslexia, but it recharged me.

Keystone rejected some of my first ideas for *Air Buddies*. I had to learn that the formula for success was to write what Robert and Anna would think kids thought was funny. They thought kids loved puns. So I wrote puns. They shot every scenario I came up with. And I was getting paid. Due to *Air Buddies*' success, a franchise was born. Keystone thought not even the sky was the limit—*Space Buddies* was the third of seven *Air Buddies* films. Over the years, I worked on most of them, doing full passes or comedy punch-ups. The pay was underwhelming. But as the sequels added up, so did my savings.

TM teaches that enlightenment can come through any vessel. It took a monkey detective to make me realize that I could possibly be a comedy writer. Years of struggling to express myself had amplified my negative opinion of my creative potential. All my life, I had been searching for something to excel at while telling myself I would never be good at professions that required reading and writing. How could I be a comedy writer when I struggled to read a takeout menu? TM gave me the tools to let those thoughts pass. I counteracted them with practice. I began to see what other people had known for years. I was funny. Not just family dinner table funny, or Oshawa basement funny, but funny enough to be asked to write a movie. Professionally funny.

And I'd been making a name for myself in the Vancouver comedy scene. Nathan and I made it to the main stage of the Vancouver Theatre, performing with the company's veterans and earning thirty dollars a pop. I had accomplished more than I thought was possible.

I knew the next stage in my life wouldn't be on a runway, but on a stage. In New York City, the Upright Citizens Brigade was hitting its stride. At least that's what Nathan said. I had been in touch with my partner in crime from the Love brothers' basement, Bum. Bum was living in New York City, trying to make it as an alt-country musician. He had an extra room in his Harlem apartment. I was welcome to stay as long as I wanted.

8

UCB/OCD

On a freezing February morning, I lugged Ronnie's trunk to the stoop of a redbrick building on East 103rd Street and rang the bell. Bum opened the door in boxers and a royal blue terry cloth bathrobe. On the back, sequins spelled out *Mr. Wonderful.*

"Nice robe."

"Right? Had this guy make it custom."

That would be Bum's response to most things. That or "I found it on eBay."

I followed Bum up four flights of stairs into an apartment with guitars hanging on every inch of wall space. Bum's home had a pawn shop aesthetic that's too often overlooked in decor magazines. Under his axe collection sat a giant television, a phone shaped like a Ferrari, and a velvet couch piled with leather pants and Vegas-era Elvis-style Western shirts.

"I took some shit out of your room," Bum explained.

Bum kicked open the door to my room. Everybody says, "My first bedroom in New York was a closet." Mine was. A windowless six-by-ten box. A child's mattress sat on the floor beneath a massive guitar amplifier. I gasped.

"Most people have that reaction," said Bum. "It's just like Keith's. That's gotta stay, I'm afraid."

I couldn't sleep that night, terrified the giant amp that was just like Keith's would topple over and make me dead, just like Brian Jones. But I had my own room in New York City. I'd dreamed of New York since the day I'd strolled through the East Village with Shalom.

———————

I took the subway to West Twenty-Third Street and walked one block to the Upright Citizens Brigade Theatre. A line stretched way up the street. Nathan had been right. I felt like I was about to be part of something.

Inside, the stage, walls, and floor were as black as a freshly tarred driveway. My classmates were just out of college. Mason had gone to Brown. Harrison, Harvard. Like Nathan, they'd studied comedy. Read all the books a young performer should read. They rattled off the titles to each other. I nodded along, hoping no one would ask my thoughts on *Truth in Comedy: The Manual of Improvisation*, which everyone seemed to have committed to memory. My classmates knew UCB's history, knew that this seventy-five-seat black box theater used to be an adult video store. All they talked about were *SNL* auditions and commercial agents and writing jobs. Though I'd already starred in commercials and earned a writing credit on a film, I felt like I was back in high school, walking into the advanced classroom straight from special ed.

When I returned to Harlem that evening, I found a crane lifting a motorbike through our window.

"It's an exact replica of Evel Knievel's," Bum said, a smoke jammed between his lips as he guided the front wheel over the windowsill. "When I was a kid, I wouldn't have believed this."

"I can't believe it now."

"Right," Bum said, nodding his cigarette up and down.

Bum bartended six nights a week at Sway, a celebrity hot spot in SoHo. He made up to a thousand bucks a shift, which he spent immediately on vintage effects pedals, Pez dispensers, architecture books, and custom gold jewelry. Forever a son of Oshawa, he smoked hash off hot knives, but now, a bohemian New Yorker, he used an antique blowtorch to heat them up.

"Can you imagine if this thing could tell stories?" he'd ask, transfixed by the blue flame.

Bum left Sway every night after 4 a.m. He headed to the bodega on the corner, waved a heavily ringed hand, and said, "Gimme me the ushe," a slice of American cheese melted inside a Jamaican beef patty. He'd grab a six-pack of Miller High Life and head uptown to fire up the antique blowtorch that remained speechless.

It wasn't just fashion and late-night calorie consumption that Bum shared with Elvis—he was a gifted musician. As a kid, Bum had played bluegrass in his dad's band and was considered a prodigy in Oshawa. In New York, he'd become a celebrity in the downtown scene by slinging drinks to the likes of Bono and buying retro daredevil memorabilia. When I left the apartment for rehearsal, I'd find Bum nursing his sixth and final High Life of the morning, mumbling that it was "the champagne of beers" and watching *The Hilarious House of Frightenstein* on VHS.

UCB class met on Saturdays on the theater's main stage. In Vancouver, we'd practiced simple improv games. UCB taught the long-form style. Scenes could run for ten minutes. If Vancouver was Kenny G, UCB was Charles Mingus. When I didn't think, when I just reacted, I earned laughs. After our fourth class, Harrison and Mason waved me over to their huddle at the back of the micro auditorium. They sat with their knees touching, conspiratorially.

"We're forming a group," Harrison said.

"So we can rehearse outside of class. You in?" asked Mason.

"I'm down."

"Any ideas on a name?" Harrison asked.

A few weeks later, the members of Earth Wind and Coleco walked into what had once been a dress shop on the Lower East Side. Audience members sat cross-legged on the floor, drinking cans of Pabst Blue Ribbon. Framed by a window where mannequins had once stood, I asked the audience for a suggestion. The following week, we performed in an old bakery just off the West Side Highway. I was on the very outskirts of show business. My modeling money was long gone. My talking chimp dough was running thin. But I felt myself improving with every show. When I walked the streets of New York, broke and tired, on my way to perform for ten people, I knew I was exactly where I needed to be.

———

One fall night, after a dress shop show, I invited Mason and Harrison to Sway. "I once saw Kelly Osbourne walk out of here when she found out how much a drink cost," I told them. "Tonight, we'll drink for free."

We found Bum behind the bar in silver leather pants and a bedazzled blouse undone to his naval. His gold lightning bolt chain swung back and forth as he shook hands.

"Harrison? Like George? Right on."

Bum handed me a cocktail shaker of shooters and flashed his fingers into metal devil horns. On the packed dance floor, models and wannabe Bums danced and posed. Harrison and Mason stood with their hands in their corduroys, like nerds who showed up uninvited to the cool kid's party, until a server grabbed my arm.

"Bum said to get you guys a booth," she said, pulling us through the crowd to a table at the edge of the dance floor.

Harrison and Mason drained the shaker and started whooping it up, sitting on top of the booth. The server dropped off a bottle of champagne. "Happy birthday," she said. Happy birthday was code for Bum has coke. I went to unwrap my gift. When I returned, two women who looked like models were seated next to Harrison and Mason.

"Sarah and Sasha here don't believe we're in Weezer," Mason said, giving me a look that said, *Yes—and. My sex life depends on it.*

"River doesn't like to be recognized," I said. "Isn't that why you're wearing contacts instead of glasses?"

"This fucking guy says he doesn't want to be recognized, then here we are," Harrison played along.

"What band are you in?" Sarah shouted over the music.

"RatDog," I said, knowing that Bob Weir's current project would put her focus back on my friends. After the bottle of champagne disappeared, Sasha and Sarah bopped into the abyss of people on the dance floor.

"Must not have been true music fans," Harrison observed.

"Yeah, good luck finding someone else who's fake-sold millions of records," I said.

Bum and I partied at Sway long after he shouted "last call" and then took a cab up to Harlem. At 7 a.m., the sun glared through the window behind Bum's gigantic TV. I left Bum to his High Lifes and passed out on my child's mattress, which Bum had nicknamed the Maxi Pad.

A shrill ringing yanked me out of my stupor. My head pounded. My mouth was bone-dry. I didn't answer. But the phone rang a second time. I staggered to the living room and picked up the Ferrari-shaped receiver.

"My beautiful Taurus and fellow Canadian," said my friend Melissa.

Like Shalom, Melissa was a living example that you never know what is around the corner for you. Melissa had been performing with her independent band Tinker in a small Montreal venue when the Smashing Pumpkins' Billy Corgan discovered her. Before she knew it, she was playing bass in Courtney Love's band Hole. Her first gig was in front of 100,000 people at the Glastonbury Festival.

"Melissa?" Hearing her voice reminded me of her two-drink rule and how I need to implement it.

"Come see me."

"When?"

"Now—222 West 23rd."

I love New York for countless reasons, but wordless addresses are at the top of my list. When I arrived, I couldn't believe my eyes— Melissa lived at the Chelsea Hotel. Her room was on the sixth floor. She gave me a tight hug. She smelled like vanilla, as always.

"It's so good to see you," she said, sitting me down on her couch and holding my hand.

"I was just thinking that about you. I can't believe you live here. The Dead played on the roof on August 10, 1967."

"I knew you'd bring that up. How are you? Tell me everything."

"I had a late one last night. Way overindulged."

"Is that why you moved to New York?"

"No," I said. "If I just wanted to party, I could have stayed in Oshawa."

I crashed at the Chelsea that night and never left. Melissa gave me the pullout couch in the living room and her bedroom when she was on tour. Bum wouldn't miss the six hundred bucks a month I paid to sleep under his guitar rig. Even though he worshipped Evel Knievel, sleeping under that amp had made me the real daredevil.

Mark Twain and Allen Ginsberg both wrote at the Chelsea. It was also where Robert Hunter wrote "Stella Blue," one of my favorite Hunter/Garcia ballads. Those of us in the neurodiversity community can relate to lyrics like "broken dreams" and "can't win for trying" at far too young an age. The Chelsea's creative energy was tangible. Ethan Hawke lived in the room beneath us. I almost skateboarded into him once when I got off on the wrong floor. My favorite people were the older tenants, the ones who'd lived in the Chelsea since Sid and Nancy roamed the halls. I walked to UCB every day to watch shows and threw myself into performing with Earth Wind and Coleco.

One day I was closing the door and heading to UCB when it hit me: Did I leave the stove on? I checked. Nope. I'd made it out the door and two steps toward the elevator before another thought bombarded me: What about the kitchen faucet? I rushed back. I was going to be late for class. Off. Another invasion took place before I hit the hall: What if, while checking the faucet, I'd inadvertently turned on the oven? After confirming that wasn't the case, I made it as far as the sidewalk before returning to ensure I'd locked the door.

I'd had obsessive tendencies since I started school. In first grade, I prayed every night that I'd wake up smart. I ended my prayers by blessing my friends and family. Then I started listing professions. All the hockey players, all the architects, all the dentists. Stuntmen, secretaries, welders. Every night, I thought of more people, more occupations. This continued until I confessed my nightly routine to my mom. "Why don't you just bless the good people of the world, sweetheart?" she suggested. Once again, Joan Hanley saved the day.

You see, dyslexia doesn't start and stop with reading and writing. It affects depth perception and organization. Without these skills, which are automatic to most people, I need to incessantly second-guess my actions. To accomplish normal tasks, like filling out a date on a form, I'm forced to obsess over what most would consider a mindless detail. To this day, I want to write September 18, 2023, and I'll bust out April 7, 2020. Or in the middle of the summer, I'll think, "Spring is around the corner."

Living in a historic artifact threw jet fuel on my rituals. I'd check each stove burner and say, out loud, "Off." Then I'd check the faucet in the kitchen: "Off." Then the faucet in the bathroom: "Off." Then back to the kitchen sink to make sure the stopper wasn't in the sink drain. That could lead to a flood. Then I'd have the compulsion to rush to the bathroom again, where it would dawn on me: maybe I brushed the dial on the stove.

Soon it took me forty-five minutes to get from my apartment to the lobby. That didn't mean I was home free. Once I reached the street, I'd often turn around and have one more kick at the can. I'd show up late to UCB, sweating and drained, mumbling excuses. It wasn't as if I could tell my colleagues, "Sorry, I've been locking and unlocking the door since dawn. You know how it is."

By summer, the bad days outnumbered the good ones. I couldn't get away from my intrusive thoughts. I was paralyzed with body-quaking anxiety. I was disappearing into my own mind, and I couldn't see a way out. On my worst days, I couldn't leave the Chelsea, terrified that I'd burn it down. One day Earth Wind and Coleco splurged and hired a veteran performer to coach us. I couldn't break the checking loop and never showed up. I found myself thinking, Man, I would kill to go back to the days when my only burden was being unable to read. I was convinced I was losing my mind.

Worried, Melissa gave me the name of a hypnotist. She worked out of her penthouse in one of the tallest buildings on the Upper East Side. The hypnotist answered the door in full Stevie Nicks regalia.

"You must be Phil," she said, unwrapping and rewrapping her black shawl.

"Thanks for seeing me."

"Don't thank me. Thank the universe for uniting us."

"Okay."

She led me to a leather recliner. I lay down and walked her through my growing list of rituals.

"How much do you know about past life regression?"

"The normal amount. None."

"Okay, close your eyes."

She told me my eyes were getting heavy. That I was falling into a state of deep relaxation. "Imagine leaving your apartment. Instead of feeling stressed and filled with compulsions, you are calm and relaxed," she said, and then counted backward from ten. When she reached "one," I would open my eyes and be cured of my compulsions. I left her apartment hopeful; I was unable to leave my own apartment later that evening.

Desperate, I found a psychiatrist and explained my behavior. She offered little insight and prescribed Zoloft, an antidepressant. I began adding meditation sessions when obsessive thoughts hit. Like an addict upping his dose, I thought more would help. I now know that "this better fix my fucking brain" is not a correct way to set your intentions before you sit. I began to feel that meditation owed me something, like a loan shark collecting from a client. I was trying to shake down my practice, telling my mind, "Give me tranquility or I'm going to break your fucking legs."

Then I remembered that Stewart had told me TM centers offered advanced classes. I needed stronger stuff. If I could evolve my practice, I could get my obsessions under control. I phoned the TM center in Manhattan and told them I wanted to enroll in advanced courses.

"Have you missed any sessions in the past twelve months?" the instructor asked me. "In other words, have you meditated for twenty minutes twice a day, every day, for the past year?"

I considered TM a sacred practice, and I felt I needed to answer with total honesty. "I've never missed a session," I said. "There were a couple I had to cut short."

"I'm sorry," he said. "But you can't take the advanced courses."

I was furious. More than that, I was despondent. I needed TM to keep me steady. It was the only thing holding me together. And they wouldn't let me progress because I'd done seventeen and a half minutes instead of twenty a couple of times?

"Fuck that," Melissa said. "You don't need their approval to get better." She told me about a Vipassana meditation retreat some of her musician friends had attended. "They said it changed their lives," she said. If I really wanted to get deeper, I should go there.

It was August and sunny when I took the bus to Shelbourne, Massachusetts. I arrived at the meditation center on "day zero" and pretended to read the intake paperwork. I handed in my cell phone and any writing tools I might've had, and I agreed to a ten-day vow of silence.

"Any reading material?" the admissions director asked.

"Not applicable," I replied.

I was assigned to the men's dormitory, which had a real still-under-construction vibe. Small unpainted plywood cubicles that slept two were housed in a large, dim gymnasium filled with identical cubicles. I put my knapsack under my single bed, fitted it with the twin sheet I'd been instructed to bring, and laid out my sleeping bag. A cocky, sporty-looking dude entered and nodded my way.

"You ready to set sail?" he asked.

I started my spiritual journey by nicknaming him "huge douche." I followed my new roommate to a giant auditorium. Seventy men sat on one side of the room. Seventy women sat on the other. An instructor dressed as a monk looked down at the meditators from an elevated platform. He told us our schedule, which would be followed down to the minute.

4:00 a.m.: Wake-Up Bell

4:30 a.m.–6:30 a.m.: Meditate

6:30 a.m.–8:00 a.m.: Breakfast

8:00 a.m.–11:00 a.m.: Meditate

11:00 a.m.–1:00 p.m.: Lunch

1:00 p.m.–5:00 p.m.: Meditate

5:00 p.m.–6:00 p.m.: Tea

6:00 p.m.–7:00 p.m.: Meditate

7:00 p.m.–8:15 p.m.: Lecture

8:30 p.m.–9:00 p.m.: Meditate

10:00 p.m.: Lights Out

My solo sessions at home were nothing compared to this. We meditated for five hours before lunch. I never realized how painful sitting with your legs crossed could be. Yet the most painful area wasn't my lower back. It was my brain, still running wild with intrusive thoughts. I remained optimistic that my thoughts and limbs would become accustomed to their new demands.

At the end of each day, we were allowed to approach the monk, one at a time, and briefly break our vow of silence to ask questions.

"What if I keep having bad thoughts?" I queried.

"No bad thoughts," he said. "You are only good thoughts."

The next morning, I resumed my bad thoughts. Without any stimulus, they were constant and unavoidable. At the end of the day, I approached the monk again with a fine-tuned question.

"What if I can't control my thoughts?"

"Don't control. Let thoughts rise and pass. Rise and pass."

By the third night, when he saw me in line, he rolled his eyes. "I keep having thoughts that are causing tremendous anxiety," I said. "I must not be doing it right."

He sighed loudly. "Your thoughts rise and pass. Everything rises and passes. Like nature." Before I could hit him with a follow-up, he bowed, which is monk for beat it, bitch.

The grueling schedule started to get to us. I was counting the days, convinced I was causing permanent damage to my knees. My sporty-looking cubicle mate started muttering to himself,

"This is bullshit. This is fucking bullshit!" and soon after that, he was gone.

On day ten our vow of silence ended. A middle-aged man from Bangladesh cornered me at the vegetarian burrito station and started telling me about how horny he got during the retreat.

"I was visited by visions of sin," he said.

I fled to my exit interview. The admissions director handed me my phone and asked, "Are you vegetarian?"

"No."

"The more you meditate, the more difficult it will be to consume life. Do you drink?"

"Yes."

"That will change," he said smugly.

I collected my twin sheet from my cubicle. The monk stood at the exit, beaming as people lined up to thank him. When it was my turn, I couldn't resist. "What do I do when I can't stop thinking thoughts I don't want to have?" I asked.

Not much for long speeches, he gave me a look that said, "I don't think this one is going to make it." On the bus ride back to the city, I chastised myself for being such a bad meditator that I'd managed to annoy a monk. Proof my mom is more patient than a monk.

———

Back in New York, I resumed my crippling compulsions. At the end of my rope, I found a new therapist. Her beige walls were covered with abstract paintings. I told her the details of my daily routine. My repetitive behaviors.

"It's pretty clear you're suffering from obsessive-compulsive disorder," she said.

"My other therapist said I was depressed."

"Your symptoms are textbook."

I'm convinced that, in my case, dyslexia led to obsessive-compulsive disorder. There isn't much research—yet, anyway—on connections between dyslexia and OCD. But there's a link between dyslexia and ADHD, and a link between ADHD and OCD, so make of that what you will. My theory is backed by exactly zero science, but I believe that my OCD was brought on by the rug being pulled out when I first found out I had a learning disability. It was the rudest of all awakenings. I picture myself happily getting ready for the first day of first grade with the sweet ignorance of someone about to die in a freak accident. Just before I enter the school doors, six-year-old me looks up, thinking, Wow, that crane is lifting that grand piano just like in the cartoons. Then . . . *That's all, folks!*

Except the cartoon didn't end. The piano crashed on my head every day for years. If you are incorrect from 8:55 a.m. to 3:20 p.m. five days a week, you will start questioning yourself. I put a tremendous amount of effort into learning to read. Practice did not make perfect. Practice led to zero out of twelve. No matter what I did, I failed. And when I reached adulthood, doom still felt unavoidable. I couldn't trust my own mind. No matter how often I checked the stove, it might be on.

I kept trying to treat my OCD through meditation. I whittled my diet down to bare essentials. I didn't drink alcohol or caffeine. After performing at UCB, I'd rush back to my apartment and meditate for hours to avoid the guilt I felt coming on for not having meditated enough that day. Sometimes I'd get home late and cram the two hours in then, staying up meditating until 3:00 a.m. Soon I was meditating to prevent something terrible from happening.

So much of meditation is intention. I intended to cure my obsessive thoughts. But I had the wrong approach. To deal with OCD, you have to get out of your head. I did the opposite: going deep into my thoughts in solitude for hours on end. Trying to fix OCD by meditating is like having a broken arm and trying to do curls to strengthen your muscles. The bone is still broken.

I finally reached a breaking point. My fanaticism about meditating and my raging OCD outweighed my drive to become a top-rate improv performer. Meditation is something I still do to this day, something that continues to help me stay balanced, focused, and driven. But at this stage in my life, it was all-consuming. My meditation cushion became a charging station for my intrusive thoughts. What I thought was the cure had become its own illness. So I did what was best for me, what I'd done before when things weren't right. I went home.

My parents at my mom's teachers college graduation in Toronto in the '60s

Me as a two-year-old on the stairs of our house in Oshawa, Ontario

My dad and I in our front yard in Oshawa

Vest Friends (me at age four)

Dark days . . . a picture says a thousand words, and I couldn't spell any of them

Postcard of Oshawa, a.k.a. the Dirty Shwa, in the '80s

Mom's Jetta, pre–Dead stickers

Patty and me on my new scooter

Bum taking care of business

Visiting Shalom on set in Toronto

My first modeling shoot, last satin shirt

First time on the runway, Dolce & Gabbana

Edged out by abs and pectorals at the Armani headquarters in Milan

MTV video award show with Patty Schemel, Courtney Love, and Melissa

Ronnie and me at the legendary Prince Bonaparte in West London

Shalom visits London

The only low-rider in town, London

First big print campaign: Dockers, baby

There's no end to my mom's patience, Vancouver

My parents in English Bay, Vancouver

Back at UCB in NYC, this time as a stand-up

Monumental day on tour: touching Jerry's axe at the Rock & Roll Hall of Fame

Marty and me in Vancouver

Shooting my comedy
special, *Ooh La La*

Working on my book
in my dad's chair,
Vancouver

9

~~Improv~~ Stand-Up Guy

I dreamed of New York but I woke up in Vancouver. Back in the spare bedroom at my parents' condo. In the en suite bathroom, I took two pills from the yellow medication organizer, a welcome home present from my mom. When my psychiatrist diagnosed me with OCD in August, she had prescribed Zoloft to help with intrusive thoughts. Then Prozac. Next, a higher dose of Zoloft. Now it was October, and they'd added Wellbutrin to the cocktail.

Nathan was picking me up at 4:45. I stayed in bed until 4:30. We drove out to a Galaxy Bowl in the sticks of British Columbia. Out the window, pines repeated in an evergreen blur. On the Trans-Canada Highway, we passed cars that brought up the past. Joshua from Oshawa's Saturn. Pugs's dad's Subaru. A blue Jetta like my mom's. A nervous breakdown makes everything but the present feel like the good old days.

"Just tell me what you got," said Nathan.

"All right, all right. But remember, I don't know what I'm doing," I insisted.

"Just tell me what you got," Nathan repeated.

"I arrived in the first grade, and everyone started reading. I was like, 'I'm going to stare out the window for a decade, but you guys do your thing.'" It was a joke from my final UCB monologue.

Nathan smiled and smacked the steering column. "That's gold. Sarcastic and snarky. It's so you. You already found your voice."

"Really? I could say that onstage and people would laugh?"

"It's better than most of the stuff stand-ups are performing around town."

"Stand-up, really? Whenever they say something, instead of laughing, I think . . . so."

"Even the way you just said that is funny. Your delivery is funny. Just get five minutes of ideas and go up and try it."

"Ideas?"

"Jokes, ideas. Just go up and talk for five minutes," said Nathan, accelerating through a bend in the highway. "Think about it. Improv needs a team. You get so frustrated when people no-show or are late for rehearsals. Stand-up is a solo sport. It's just you up there."

I'd never given stand-up any thought. Never fell in love with a parent's collection of Pryor or Carlin records. But I started to hear Nathan's reasoning. At UCB, I'd worked with people who had college degrees, real jobs, and relationships that they had the luxury of prioritizing. People with choices. People who didn't have to have my all-in attitude. And why would they? They could read, write, and function normally. My commitment was rooted in my lack of options. As a stand-up, I knew I would be there. And something about improv felt stifling. The part I didn't control. If my scene partner said I was a one-armed ostrich surgeon, I had to be on board. I had no choice but to tuck an arm behind my back and respond, "Gimme a hand getting this bad boy on the table."

———

I started writing out joke ideas. I began with "It's unfair that the short bus is half the size of a regular bus but has the same number of flashing lights and signs." I went for a walk on the seawall, the waterfront path that lines the city, trying to outstep my dark thoughts. I stopped and scribbled on a scrap of paper, "It's like arriving at school in a winning slot machine."

The next afternoon, while lying in bed, I had an idea about emailing a woman to ask her out, misspelling a word, and offending her. I quickly wrote it down. Then it was back to my regularly scheduled programming: OCD.

The next time I saw Nathan, I brought six pages of material on a yellow legal pad. It was spaced every other line so I could read my own writing. Nathan listened to my ideas and recommended comedians who fit my style. I loved Todd Barry's dry and deadpan delivery. Dave Attell was so fast on his feet. Nathan took me to see the documentary *Comedian*, about Jerry Seinfeld. I followed Seinfeld around New York City as he built a new hour of material. By the time the credits rolled, I was in.

Trying stand-up comedy was my only glimmer of hope. I was sleeping sixteen hours a day. My parents woke me up only for doctors' appointments. My dad always drove. Our family practitioner referred me to an OCD specialist at the University of British Columbia. Dr. Whittdal was friendly. She smiled, revealing a perfect ratio of gums to teeth.

"What medication have you been prescribed?" she asked.

I reached both hands into the black army pants I wore every day in high school and pulled out handfuls of orange bottles. They formed a mound on the table. Dr. Whittdal's eyes got wide.

"They're really leaving no stone unturned," she said, writing down each medication. Wellbutrin, ratio-fluoxetine, clonazepam, Rhovane, Risperdal, apo-divalproex, Zyprexa, paroxetine, Seroquel, Frosst, Zoloft, Paxil. "What are you currently taking?" she asked. "You can't be taking all this at once."

"Paxil, Wellbutrin, another I can't read the name of, and a sleeping pill that I also can't read the name of. It starts with a Z and it's blue."

"I have to ask," Dr. Whittdal said, clicking her pen closed. "Are you having thoughts of hurting yourself?"

I held my breath. When I exhaled, I confessed. "I've been thinking about killing myself a lot. It's weird. It gives me comfort. Planning it out methodically soothes me. I do it while I'm trying to fall asleep. It's like a goth lullaby."

Dr. Whittdal nodded. I continued.

"I'm going to swallow a bottle of prescription sleeping pills. The ones I can't read the name of. Then wash it down with margarita mix and polar ice vodka. Chug it. I always picture doing it at that hostel on the edge of Gastown called the Cambie."

Dr. Whittdal knew the place.

"No idea why I picked it. I guess I figured if you're going to kill yourself, why not ruin an Australian's trip?"

When I got to the end of the scenario, I realized I might not get to go home. I looked down at the brown carpet.

"Do you think it's likely that you will execute your plan?"

I caught her eye. "Absolutely not."

The truth was I'd been walking to the Cambie at night. The night before, I'd gone in and asked the bartender if they had private rooms. I sat at the bar, drank a warm bottle of Moosehead beer, and pictured walking up the stairs. I didn't picture walking back down.

———

I lingered at the side stage at the Jupiter. The cavernous restaurant bar was filled with round tables and giant leather chairs. Thirty people in attendance were scattered around the room, some with their backs to the stage. The host was not fazed. His blow job pantomime was just hitting its stride. Morgan's gray goatee twitched under his bald head as he reached the climax. The audience hadn't settled into foreplay.

Morgan's caramel tan reminded me of the Giusti boys. His trick, he'd told me, was to sunbathe through the winter at a nude beach. "Okay, our first act is brand-new, he's never done stand-up before and he's an improv guy," Morgan told the crowd. "So let's be nice to him—because he's not really a stand-up, he's an improv guy. Here he is, the improv guy, Phil Hanley!"

I walked onstage, took the microphone out of the stand, and launched into the material I had spent weeks memorizing. Time seemed to speed up while I performed. I told a joke that referenced Mr. T. It got a laugh. I talked about being dyslexic and joked about hating the Adidas short shorts that men wore when I was a kid because I claimed to have a nut allergy. After my set, Morgan returned to the stage, shouting, "I think we have a winner! Keep it going for him! He's an improv guy! Phil Hanley! He's an improv guy!"

I'd stepped offstage and was walking to where my sister, Patty, was seated at the back of the room. As the crowd applauded, I understood the concept of love at first sight. My next thought was: How can I get back onstage? Within seconds of doing my first stand-up set, I knew it was what I wanted to do for the rest of my life. I had found the thing I'd been searching for. The thing that came to me the way reading had come to my classmates.

Morgan ran another show at a bar called DV8. The stage was on the ground level, circled by balconies. The comics hung out up there before their sets, figuratively and literally looking down on the other performers. Patty came along, but I sat at a table by myself. We'd always been close. She had even visited me when I lived in England. But I had pushed her away since I'd come home. Patty refused to accept that I wanted to be alone. The more she insisted, the more I receded. Repelling her kindness was evidence of how sick I was.

Morgan dropped two small paper tickets in front of me. I looked up, confused.

"It's drink tickets for doing the show," he said. "You get two free drinks. Well, you're only allowed to order draft beer."

I thanked him, but I knew that alcohol wouldn't mix well with all the medication marinating my brain. I went back to silently rehearsing my jokes. I had written them down on a page from my yellow legal pad. No one except me could have deciphered a word. I'd begin writing the word *appreciate*, reach the *p*, and freestyle the rest. I understood it by its shape. And I was the only one who had to read it. I knew what these words meant and how they fit together because, suddenly, they were mine.

A comic I recognized from the Jupiter took the empty chair. "Hey, I'm Peter Reed. I saw your set last week," he said. "I loved that Adidas bit. I told my wife. She laughed her ass off." Peter eyed my set list. "It's nice to see someone take it seriously out of the gate. Vancouver's tough. There's not a ton of stage time. I mean, you have to get up five times a week to ever get funny."

I nodded.

Walking home, I told Patty I didn't think the set went well. "Are you kidding me?" she asked. "You seemed more comfortable, and I love the changes you made."

Peter's words stuck in my head. Five shows a week seemed impossible. I was determined to do it. I got home that night, pinned a piece of paper to my bedroom wall, and drew two hash marks, the way prisoners in movies count days behind bars. I saw it as a way out. Each notch was a step toward New York. And one step further from the Cambie.

10

Get Up, Stand Up

At the Backstage Lounge open mic in Vancouver, a middle-aged man in khakis sawed a violin bow across his black Les Paul to a prerecorded Led Zeppelin track. Ten minutes later, the music cut in the middle of his solo. He packed up his gear as a singer-songwriter named Raven took the stage. There was no audience. Just eight other wannabe musicians and me waiting our turns.

"Nexxxt uppp we got comedy stylings from the twisted mind of Phil Hanley," the sound guy announced over the PA.

My mind wasn't twisted, not as far as he knew. And why did he give Mister Rogers Marilyn Manson's intro? A perfect opener, as I was wearing my favorite blue cardigan, a gift from Ronnie. I ignored my instinct and went right into a rehearsed bit: "I'm from Oshawa, Ontario, which is like Detroit minus the European flair."

Silence. It bombed. I bombed.

Why hadn't I trusted my gut? I would have instantly connected with people who had been getting bad introductions from the same guy every Monday night for years. No matter. I didn't care how hard I had just bombed, or how few people were in the audience. I was in it. Doing five minutes in front of ten people meant more than walking the runway for Giorgio Armani before scores of celebrities. Modeling was something I had fallen into. Stand-up was something I truly and passionately wanted to chase. I had to get good.

Vancouver wasn't exactly a comedy hot spot. It's the most isolated major city in Canada. With limited venues, I got creative. I followed any Joan Baez tribute act the Vancouver music scene threw at me. I performed between bands as they set up and tuned their instruments. I did ambush comedy nights at restaurants. Referring to these as shows is misleading. It's like calling a smash-and-grab robbery a shopping spree. People weren't anticipating comedy. They wanted to enjoy their meal. And we would spring a show on them the way an alligator attacks an antelope at a watering hole, only with dick jokes.

"Are you dyslexic, sir?" I asked a guy sitting with his back to the stage during an early gig at an Italian restaurant.

"No."

"You're impossible to connect with."

The laugh from this exchange held the audience's attention for the rest of the joke. Short windows of attentiveness forced me to write concise jokes that were precisely worded. When I wrote my jokes out—and let's be honest, they were more scribbled—my goal was to have a laugh every three lines on my legal pad, which is about every fifteen words. If I went over fifteen words, I needed two laughs back-to-back. For a dyslexic brain that specializes in big-picture thinking, this detail-oriented method was difficult. But for me, *everything* is difficult, so what was the difference? Getting to the punch line quickly was essential.

———

"Are you sure about this?" asked my dad as he put his car in neutral.

"It'll be fine," I said. "Thanks for the ride."

I headed into the bar of the Cobalt Motor Hotel, one of the "crack hotels" in Vancouver's Downtown Eastside. Canada's poorest postal code. The bar on the ground floor served as a clubhouse for the city's homeless gutter punk population, whom Vancouverites often called squeegee kids because they raised money by offering to clean windshields at stop lights.

I had been to the Cobalt once before with Nathan to see a Black Sabbath cover band called Sack Blabbath. We left when a fight broke out after a woman with blue dreads threw a beer stein at the singer.

"Is there a sign-up sheet?" I asked a bored bartender.

He tapped his tattooed finger against his shaved head.

"My name's Phil."

"You're next, Bill. Just plug into the house PA."

"Oh, I'm a comedian."

"Ouch. Whatever, you're next."

I stood at the back of the room. No one was paying attention to the thrash metal two-piece onstage. Two pit bulls fought over a knotted sock. The room smelled bad, like I imagined a mushroom farm might: fungus spores and manure. I noticed that the large support beam in the middle of the room was painted with the names of musicians who had died. I spotted Jerry Garcia's name and felt guilty for being judgmental. The bartender collected glasses nearby and I shouted over the music: "I like the Jerry memorial."

"Memorial? Those are people we're glad are dead."

An MC with a mohawk and a '70s plaid suit appeared onstage. "Next up comedian . . . Bill," he announced. "He better be funny."

I looked straight ahead over the pit bulls and delivered my act to the back wall. Without any laughs, jokes become a run-on sentence. I couldn't find my rhythm. I thought I had bombed before. This was a new low. An atomic bomb.

As I recited my act, I noticed the woman who'd thrown a beer stein at Sack Blabbath. She had her blue dreads tied up in a giant bun. "Last time I was here she chucked a beer stein at Ozzy Osbourne," I riffed, earning my first laugh.

She stamped her foot and shouted, "Fuck you, Bill. And your gay cardigan."

Everyone cheered.

"That hurts coming from punk rock Marge Simpson."

The room crackled with laughter and energy. My set went from being dead in the water to a living, breathing thing. Everyone was invested; even the pit bulls ignored their sock. Then something hit my shoulder. The sudden flood of adrenaline made it impossible to assess the damage. Did Marge hit me with a beer stein? Why didn't I hear it smash on the ground? I got hit again in the same spot. I was under attack and they were aiming for my head. Looking down I saw a wad of wet toilet paper glistening on the stage. The crowd cheered.

"Woo Ashtray."

"Ashtray, Bill's pissed."

I gathered the assailant's name was Ashtray. The mic trembled in my hand. I tried to compute my next move. Instinctually, I went into a bit. "I'm used to it. When I was a kid, I used to have to take the short bus. I'm dyslexic with a capital Q."

The host flicked a flashlight on and off. My time was up. I put the mic back in the stand. Ashtray waited for me by the side of the stage. I clenched my fists and stepped toward him, prepared to fight. Ashtray stretched out his arms. His smile revealed where most of his teeth used to be, and why he was called Ashtray.

"I'm sorry. Marge Simpson is my girl," he said, gripping me in a hug.

I got home buzzing and found my dad watching TV. "How did it go?" he asked. "I hated dropping you off at that dump."

"It was fine."

"You had a good set?"

"Good in a weird way."

"What does that mean?"

"Weird but . . . good?"

"Thanks for clearing that up, Delph."

My dad was watching a documentary about captive elephants. Poachers traveled deep into the jungles of Central Africa in search of elephants that had never laid eyes on humans. They stole adolescent elephants from their mothers, tied their limbs to trees, and slapped and poked them with sticks twenty-four hours a day. After seven days, the broken animals could be trained to haul logs.

"This is brutal," my dad said.

I agreed. But I also saw a parallel to stand-up comedy. Making a room full of strangers laugh is as unnatural as an elephant working in the lumber industry. Like them, I was experiencing exposure therapy. Getting poked and prodded until I was able to do my job.

The next time I performed at the Cobalt, I had a drummer play a beat behind my jokes. It made me realize the importance of rhythm in stand-up. The gutter punks didn't throw any more objects. One of them invited me to the Cobalt Christmas party, where the activities included bobbing for joints in an old bedpan.

———

A few weeks later, I arrived at a small bar with blackout curtains on the windows. The only light came from tea candles. My eyes adjusted. Middle-aged people lined the bar and sat on a long sofa. They were suspiciously dressed up. I hadn't seen people in evening attire since New York. In Vancouver, people referred to their black Patagonia as their dressy fleece. A guy with outdated glasses materialized out of the darkness and stuck out his hand.

"Hi, I'm Randy. You must be Phil."

"Thanks for having me," I said. Everyone was staring at us.

"Morgan gave you the details?"

"Ten minutes."

"If you want to help me with the raffle afterward, be my guest. I figure you could just do it over there." Randy pointed to the small patch of wall between the washrooms at the end of the bar. Then he leaned in so close that his breath moved my hair. "Don't mention the swinger thing."

He cupped his hands over his mouth and yelled, "Ladies and gentlemen, Phil . . ." He paused and looked at me.

"Hanley."

"Handley!"

I started: "I'm from Oshawa, Ontario, which is like Detroit . . ."

A woman in a shimmering gown slapped her knee. "I'm from Whitby, honey."

A town hall meeting started. My female constituents were on board. Their male counterparts were not. They sat with their arms crossed. Ten minutes was the longest set I had ever done. I needed to speak slowly, which felt counterintuitive. Your brain falsely tells you that the quicker you speak, the sooner the set will be over. I promised myself I would riff before my closer, a mediocre joke where I compared my skinny physique and beard to a Chewbacca Pez dispenser. I spotted a fishbowl of condoms on the bar. "I don't need those," I said. "My cardigan is a powerful contraceptive." My impromptu line got the biggest laugh of the set, and I said good night.

As I headed for the door, Randy announced, "Let's see who wins the incredible magic wand vibrator."

I cabbed to El Cocal, Vancouver's alt-comedy room. Two spots in one night. I felt like Seinfeld in *Comedian*, hopping from club to club. At El Cocal, I found Peter at the bar. He'd donned a robe, sandals, and a fake beard.

"I'm Jesus," he said.

"I heard you were coming back."

"I've got all this killer new religion stuff. It just poured out of me."

The host announced: "Next up, coming to the stage . . . the Chosen One."

"That's my new intro," whispered Peter, beaming. He snaked his way between the tables with his arms outstretched.

I didn't want to play a character. My stand-up was about telling people who I was and what I had experienced, an opportunity I hadn't had in school, modeling, or improv. Not only could I be myself, it was essential. Peter had that same realization. Within a couple minutes, he was flop sweating, clenching his fake beard in his hand, and asking the crowd, "What else is going on? Is anyone celebrating anything?"

My first paid gig was a matinee in a boardroom in an office building in downtown Vancouver. I opened for a comic named Watermelon, who also worked as a pinup cannabis model. When we arrived at the gig, we were brought into the boardroom. I stood at the head of the long door and performed my jokes with a whiteboard as my backdrop. A group of eight executives sat around a long table, staring at me with blank faces. The feeling of confusion was mutual. After five minutes, Watermelon took her place standing at the head of the table. As she began, the birthday boy slid his chair out and positioned himself like he was expecting a lap dance.

"It's not that type of show, buddy."

"Oh, come on, it's my birthday."

"I'll make it impossible for you to have kids if you don't close your legs," Watermelon shot back. She then proceeded to roast him and the whole situation in general. I found the office environment and the overhead lighting intimidating. Watermelon leaned into it.

Comedy is a by any means necessary craft. If you're going to fail, do it with your guns blazing. A lesson far more valuable than the twenty dollars I was paid.

———

When *Comedian* came out on DVD, it became my visual bible. Every night, with my nerves in mind, my mom would prepare an easy-to-digest dinner. She'd sip her tea and ask me, "Are you sure that's not too bland, dear?"

Once I convinced her I loved plain chicken, we would sit together in worship and watch Seinfeld work the New York City clubs—Caroline's, Gotham, and the holy grail, the Comedy Cellar. I watched the documentary the way a football coach watches game film, scrutinizing every second to glean clues or insight into how to be a better comedian. The soundtrack included Bob Dylan's "When I Paint My Masterpiece." The Dead covered that song, and I've been inspired by the lyrics since the first time I heard it. It made me believe that I too would someday create a masterpiece. Its presence on the soundtrack compounded the inspiration I got from the film.

"I haven't seen you enjoy something on repeat like this since Uncle Lee got you that Beatles album when you were five," my mom said. "You drove us crazy with that thing."

Seinfeld workshopped bits with Colin Quinn at a table at the Olive Tree Cafe, above the Comedy Cellar. It was like watching Superman and Batman talk shop. "It blows my mind that even these guys struggle to figure it out," I'd tell my mom between bites. These spirited conversations about material didn't happen in Vancouver, where opportunities were few and far between. The veterans in the scene were disenchanted. Their lessons were cautionary tales. Their names were often followed by "he used to be so funny." I was eager to get good and get out.

Without a mentor, I did something I never thought I'd do. I turned to books. I went to every bookstore in Vancouver and bought any book about comedy I could get my hands on. I forced myself to read about the Marx Brothers and W. C. Fields. The Marx Brothers had once gotten stiffed by a booker and couldn't afford train tickets to the next show. So they walked. Hell gigs were tradition. Struggles were signposts. This was the way it was supposed to be. This is how you got better.

Reading never got easier. But over time, I built stamina. I had no judgment about my pace and learned to appreciate my agonizing approach to digesting words. I lived in the scenes on the page longer than someone who could fly through a book. It's the difference between running through a forest and camping. After my mom and I both read *Harpo Speaks!* I remembered details that didn't stick with her.

I may have been reading more than ever, but that doesn't mean the alphabet and I were on friendly terms. The letter *H* was still a bastard. I still looked at books on the shelf as if they were sworn enemies. These books contained something I wanted—information— but they wouldn't give it to me for some stupid reason. So I tried to appease them. I tried to make nice with language, to say, "Hey, let's work together here. I'm not such a bad guy."

To this day, the English language ignores my sweet nothings.

Say I'm sending a text and want to use a word I haven't memorized. I misspell it, and my iPhone doesn't have any clue what I'm trying to type, so autocorrect is out of the question. So fine, I say, "Siri, how do you spell *psychology?*" And when I get the answer, my first reaction is "are you fucking serious?" I'm enraged. It's like I'm a degenerate gambler betting on a football game, and the star running back fumbles and is subject to all the profanity I can throw at it. I mean, seriously, *psychology?* What sense does that make? And naturally, *H* is still involved.

———————

Zach Galifianakis sat at a piano, wearing a tweed sport coat that looked slept in. His beard was overgrown, his hair wild, like a deranged professor on a bender. Galifianakis played chords, staring at the ceiling. He let the music drift, then delivered a hilarious short setup/punch line joke. I wanted to craft material that sharp and concise.

Galifianakis jumped up from the piano and walked out the door of El Cocal with the microphone in hand. Out of sight, he observed, "So . . . outside is weird." I'd never seen a comic so ambivalent, strange, and unpredictable.

After the show, Galifianakis joined me at a sticky table. "Is this beer for the comics?" he asked.

"Yeah, I think so."

He poured a glass, slid it over to me, and started drinking directly from the pitcher. "Are you new?" he asked.

"Just over a year."

"The audience has to get to know you quickly," Galifianakis advised, "so that they'll understand what is funny about you." He compared a stand-up's relationship with the audience to that of someone and their friends. I listened, trying to avoid touching the contaminated table. Galifianakis noticed.

"Are you germophobic?"

"Yeah, kinda."

"See, that's funny. If you were out for dinner with your friends and the waiter wiped his nose with his hand, they'd crack up. They'd know you were obsessing about his disease-ridden hand touching your plate. That it was killing you."

I realized that's why archetypes exist in comedy. When a jolly fat guy grabs the mic, the audience automatically thinks of John Candy, John Belushi, Chris Farley, and Louie Anderson. They'll laugh the second he hints at excess. Vancouver's audiences knew nothing about me. I was a skinny white dude in a city teeming with skinny white dudes. I needed to establish an identity the audience could recognize while performing deeply personal material. I had to dig deep and draw on what I had experienced. And there was a lot to draw from.

At show number 175, I opened with "I'm not only a comedian, I'm also a stay-at-home son."

Morgan saw me tell that joke at Jupiter. He waved me over to his table, where Peter sat eating hot wings. "One of my rooms, Zizanie, needs a host," he said.

"I'm available."

"Phil, I know you're available. You do twelve to fifteen minutes.

Warm up the crowd. Bring up the comics. Then light them and tell me if anyone goes long. Can you handle it?"

"No problem."

I walked out into the night air. Jubilant, I crossed out onto the Burrard Street Bridge. It had been raining and the puddles reflected the streetlights. Then a cruiser pulled over and two cops stepped out.

"How you doing tonight?" asked a cop.

"I'm good," I said, meaning it for the first time in months. "Is there a problem?"

"You tell us. There's been some break-ins and you fit the description of the suspect. Do you have some ID?"

I handed the cop my ID and he went back to the cruiser. I hadn't been stopped by the police since I was a teenager. If I was arrested, it would go on my record and prevent me from entering the States. I stared at a puddle until he returned from the cruiser.

"How was Christmas?" he asked.

"Like six months ago? Good, festive."

"There was a missing person report filed on you on December 23. Someone was worried you were going to hurt yourself."

"Well, clearly unjustly. I'm fine."

He handed me my ID.

"You need a lift home?"

"I was enjoying the walk."

With that, he was on his way. When I got home my mom was wrapping up her puttering for the day.

"I just got stopped by the cops," I said.

She stopped wiping down the counter. "You what, dear?"

"They told me someone had filed a missing person report at Christmas," I said, pissed.

"We were all worried you were going to hurt yourself. You kept disappearing. That day you'd been gone for thirteen hours."

"What if I had something on me? Can you imagine? What the hell were you guys thinking?"

"On you? What do you mean, dear?"

"Like I don't have enough to deal with, and now cops are in the mix? I'm going to bed."

———

When I arrived at Zizanie, I found the smallest restaurant I'd ever seen. And that wasn't the worst part. It was French Canadian. I never even realized this community existed in Vancouver. I had unknowingly committed to entertaining people who A) did not want to be entertained, and B) did not speak English or seemingly care for people who did.

I quickly went through my material, only to see that none of the comedians I'd invited had showed up. I needed to stretch. With my joke canteen bone-dry, I attempted to do crowd work. "Hi," I said to two women gabbing in French at a table near the stage. "Would you mind not chitchatting while I'm pursuing my dream?"

"We're catching up. We weren't anticipating a show," one of the women replied in a French accent.

"'Weren't,' past tense. You're quite a flirt," I responded. "You have a beautiful accent. I have a thing for Romanian women."

She softened. "French."

"French. My ex-girlfriend was French. She was the love of my life. That's what I'm going to say about you someday."

I can trace my ability to do crowd work to being called on in class by a teacher who wanted my thoughts on a reading assignment that I hadn't even attempted to do. I had to be quick on my feet and have faith that if I started talking something would come out. I would like to add crowd work to the list of things dyslexics excel at.

With Zizanie to run as my own room, I suddenly had hours of stage time to fill. I gave spots to comics who made me laugh. Patty came every week and brought her friends. Strangers who spoke English started showing up. People started coming back. I couldn't repeat material, so I made the show about them. I'd get details about their lives and riff with them between acts. One night, I asked a woman if she'd ever heard of dyslexia.

"I've read about it," she replied.

"You read about it? Wow. That's kind of a mean thing to say to a dyslexic. I'm sure you've heard this before, but you're a bully."

My tedious writing on the legal pad was paying off, giving me the space to riff. No two performances at Zizanie were the same. Each show became as unique as the spelling of the words it consisted of.

———

A year to the day since I had first stepped onstage at the Jupiter, I walked to St. Paul's Hospital with my mom. I remembered our journeys to the children's hospital in Toronto, where doctors had stuck needles in my head. The needles had fed information to a machine that resembled a polygraph. The printouts hadn't produced any insight into why I couldn't read.

Dr. Sharfman was the most esteemed psychiatrist in Vancouver, the head of his department at the hospital. He leaned back in his chair with his hand resting on his forehead. "How much are you sleeping?" he asked.

"Most of the day."

"And you're having thoughts of hurting yourself?"

"Yes," I said, feeling awful for my mom. And I didn't care for the hand on the forehead thing.

"Low moods?"

"After my nervous breakdown?" I asked.

"He's been very troubled for a year or so," added my mom.

"Obsessive and intrusive thoughts?"

"Yes, I've always had obsessive compulsions. But nothing like this."

"Any relief?"

"Meditation, I think. Sometimes."

"He's very depressed," my mom said. "We are worried he's been prescribed so many different drugs it has exacerbated everything."

After five minutes of questions and zero eye contact, Dr. Sharfman declared I was bipolar.

"Bipolar?" I asked. My leg started shaking. My mom put her hand on my knee.

"He doesn't have high highs or low lows," my mom said. "He's really . . ."

The doctor interrupted her. "It can manifest as a slight elevation within the low. I'm certain of the diagnosis. I'm prescribing 300 mg of lithium three times a day, and I want you to come back in three weeks." Then he finally looked up.

We weren't out of the hospital before I said, "I'm not bipolar."

"I know, dear."

"And what was that about you can have a slightly elevated low? These people have no idea what they're talking about."

"Bipolar doesn't seem right. I just don't see it."

On the walk home, I decided I wasn't taking lithium. And I was coming off everything else.

The next couple of months were a blur. I had felt awful on the medication. I felt even worse coming off it. It was like a miserable marriage followed by a drawn-out divorce. I had horrible insomnia and slept until the late afternoon. I'd wake up exhausted and nauseated. After a lifetime of making up fake illnesses to get out of school, I had them all at once. My mom would slowly open my door at dinnertime.

"Are you going to come up for something to eat?"

My parents never chided me about my odd sleep hours or dark moods. They never suggested that I snap out of it. The same way they were never hard on me about my grades.

In the evenings, I walked to Zizanie or open mics. My limbs were reluctant to listen to my brain's instructions. They seemed disconnected from my body. My bones felt waterlogged. I couldn't feel my feet when they touched the sidewalk. When comics said hello to me, their voices sounded like they came from behind a thick pane of glass.

But I always went up to the microphone. When the show started, adrenaline eased the misery. Stand-up had been my light at the end of the tunnel, my only hope of getting back to New York. Now it became the light at the end of the microtunnels that made up each day. A faint light, but one that kept me onstage five or six nights a week.

Eventually, I stopped waiting for my mom to appear in my doorway. I started coming upstairs at dinnertime. And we started watching *Comedian* again. We had moved on to the DVD extras. Listening to Colin Quinn and Seinfeld chat about comedy made me feel like it was us three hanging out.

I kept drawing the hatch marks after every show, and I kept a journal, writing detailed descriptions. Show 432: *Five people super dead and I ripped it up. There was some weird thing when this dude took a call and I told him I would use his phone as a suppository. I don't know what got into me.* Show 615: *I was really nervous like-big-time-boi. But the crowd was big and I rocked it. I felt comfortable and did some crowd work with these Australian and New Zealand guys. It sucks I can't deliver the modeling bit with gusto.* Show 709: *Interesting very interesting. I went second from the end and did a good job. I did my new bits. Some worked better than others. Then I started my crowd work and I got the biggest response. It was a guy's birthday and I claimed he was eleven. I got an applause break. Graham afterward said what a special talent crowd work like that was and how I should make it my act.* Show 780: *Wow I normally don't wow but it was a great set. I'm opening for Paul Bae and afterward he came into the greenroom gushing that I was going places. He kept saying that all my jokes are worded perfectly. Then he*

*corrected himself and said most are. He said I wouldn't be opening up for
him long. He said I should be headlining.* Show 836: *It was fun. I walked
in and Graham brought me up. I didn't even have a chance to put my bag
down. I riffed on having to wear my coat and just had fun. Lately experiencing a newfound sense of confidence. Rob Pue said how perfect I was for
TV. He said I should be thinking about what I'm going to do after I do all
the TV stuff. He said I would be hard-pressed to not win the homegrown
competition at JFL.* Show 870: *Holy shit tickets crap man. That show
sucked worse than any I've done since the Backstage Lounge. But it's a
weird kind of shitty 'cause I didn't really give a fuck.* I always returned
home to a note from my mom saying, "I hope you had a good show."
I glued them to the inside cover of my show journal.

I hit a thousand shows. Then I strove to hit fifteen hundred. I'd
do three nightmare sets in a row, honing a new bit, then crush in
front of a hot audience. I wasn't used to seeing effort translate to
improvement. As a kid, no matter how many hours I spent at the
kitchen table with my mom, reading and writing never got easier.
As a model, I lifted weights and ate mashed potatoes for breakfast
and stayed bone-skinny. Stand-up was the first thing that the more
I put into it, the more I got out. My entire life was a tightly coiled
spring. Stand-up released the tension, and I sprang forward with
decades of repressed energy. I could feel myself getting mighty.

And one night, I was hanging out in front of Zizanie, and Robin
Williams walked up in jeans and a black polo shirt.

"Hi, I'm Robin," he said in a soft voice. "Are you the host?"

"I am," I said. "Phil."

"I heard this is a fun room. Do you mind if I do a spot?"

"Of course. When do you want to go up? I'll put you on whenever."

"Oh, I'll go up at the end," he insisted. "I don't want to bump anyone or cut anyone's time."

I kept my hosting duties tight, only doing a few jokes between comics. "I used to do acid," I said. "I regret it so much. Because someday I'm going to have kids. I'll have to sit them down and explain they are the second-best thing that ever happened to me."

When I went out to get the next comic, Williams caught my eye. "I love that acid joke," he said. "So funny."

Williams hung out for over two hours, chatting with comics on the sidewalk and popping in to get a read on the room. Word got out, and for the first time, every seat in the restaurant was taken. Then a standing crowd formed. I could see Morgan's face in the window to the kitchen where the servers fetched the food.

"Ladies and gentlemen," I said. "Robin Williams."

The place exploded. Williams murdered for an hour in a bedroom-size makeshift comedy club. He swung for the fences, sweat pressing through his black shirt as he annihilated. I didn't know it at the time, but that material would become his next HBO special. And I got to see it live at the smallest restaurant in western Canada.

11

Planes, Trains, and Automobiles

The Vancouver Yuk Yuk's sat in the basement of a hotel, across the street from St. Paul's Hospital, where I was diagnosed as bipolar. On a Tuesday night in October, Yuk Yuk's showroom was half-full of people who'd paid a dollar for their seats and committed to a two-drink minimum. The house lights were low. So was the ceiling. Laughter evaporates in bright rooms with high ceilings. You want dark and tight: key elements for comedy combustion. And square tables, not round. Not overly comfortable chairs. Yuk Yuk's checked all the boxes.

On the wall behind the stage hung a sign that read International Stand-Up Comedy in yellow letters circling the words "Mark Breslin's Yuk Yuk's." Yuk Yuk's was the only comedy club in town. They operated a chain of comedy clubs across Canada, and it was the lifeblood of Canadian comics. I'd managed to land a spot on Yuk Yuk's amateur night. If I had a strong set, their booker might take notice. I wanted to stand out. No, I needed to stand out. I was four years into comedy and five into living with my parents.

The night was called Crash and Burn. If your set took a turn for the worse, the screen would project videos of planes crashing from the sky, and yes, this was post 9/11, and no, the imaging didn't help turn the set around. The first comic made it two minutes before they cued the carnage.

"Woo! Crash and burn, baby," yelled a dude in a Tapout T-shirt.

"These animals are bloodthirsty," I whispered to the doorman.

"That's my buddy," he said, smiling.

I went to the greenroom behind the stage and leafed through a mess of papers from my yellow legal pad. I knew exactly what I was going to say. I'd timed out exactly five minutes of jokes. My nerves sent my OCD into overdrive, and I felt the need to write out my set list over and over.

No infernos appeared on the screen during my set. The Tapout community remained silent. The booker offered me a guest spot on a non-apocalypse-themed show at Yuk Yuk's the following Thursday. This meant bigger exposure, more time, and a coveted set in front of an audience who paid to see comedy in a room designed for comedy. Those things were completely new to me. I'd been performing in places that were equivalent to learning to drive on black ice.

During the guest spot, I saw the headliner watching me. John Wing was in his late forties. He always wore the same outfit onstage, a gray suit and red polka-dot bow tie. After the show, he approached me.

"Good bit about living with your parents," he said in a gruff voice.

John's story was both aspirational and cautionary. He was a Canadian who had accomplished the tough task of breaking into the American comedy scene. He had done *The Tonight Show* half a dozen times. He had even gotten invited over to sit down with Johnny. Aspirational. He moved to Los Angeles, where *Tonight Show* appearances didn't turn him into a sitcom star, and now found himself back in Vancouver. Cautionary. No matter. He liked my jokes.

"I have two weekends coming up at Yuk Yuk's in Calgary and Edmonton," John said. "Is all your stuff that clean?"

For the first time, I'd be a touring, paid comedian. I'd perform before new fans outside of Vancouver. I'd have my name featured alongside a true, professional comedian who'd appeared in the biggest markets in the United States. It was only two cities, and I'd have to pay my own way there and cover my hotels on the off nights. The compensation for the gigs would barely cover the expenses. But that didn't matter. As far as I saw it, I was now a professional comic.

After thousands of shows in Vancouver, I'd get to take part in the grand tradition of going on the road. The books I struggled to read romanticized the road. For most people, the challenge began and ended with honing their act until they were good enough for a headliner to take notice. For a dyslexic, it was just the beginning. Making a group of strangers laugh was much easier than booking flights and hotels. After completely screwing it up, I asked my mom for help.

"That's why airlines give a twenty-four-hour grace period,

dear," she said. "People get the dates wrong all the time. Get the calendar from the kitchen. It will take us no time."

"I'm an idiot. Wrong date. Wrong airport."

"Well, we caught it in time. Those airport codes are tricky, to say the least. When are you flying to Edmonton?"

"December fifth. Then I take the bus to Calgary on the eighth."

"If you want, I can call Sheila. She's a great travel agent."

"Let's just do it on here," I said, hitting buttons on my desktop Gateway computer before giving up and switching places with my mom. She booked the flights in minutes.

Before I left for Edmonton, I went to a bar in Kitsilano, just over the bridge from my parents' house, where veteran comic Brent Butt hosted two sold-out shows every week. I noticed Butt told three short, killer jokes up front. Established he was funny and that people had made the right choice coming to the show. Next, he'd dip into the crowd and talk to them for a few minutes. This made the show feel unique, not another cookie-cutter performance. Then he'd do seven minutes of material to get the audience in the rhythm of jokes and the idea that if they listened to a setup, they'd be rewarded with a punch line.

My flight was on Thursday morning. Packing commenced Tuesday. For dyslexics, organization requires the precision of a commander planning a Navy SEAL mission. I tried to simplify the process by always wearing the same thing onstage. Three nights of shows meant three versions of the same outfit. I printed my tickets, went over the times and dates with the intensity of an archaeologist studying an ancient treasure map, and placed them in a backpack dedicated exclusively to travel. Hotel itineraries, bus station addresses, and contacts at the clubs were written out by my mom in her legible handwriting, filed in a manila envelope, then zipped in a specific pocket. These were my insurance policies against dyslexia. If one of these items wound up lost, so would I.

The night before my flight, I placed my bags in front of the front door. I laid out my clothes and put my wallet in my pocket. When my alarm went off, I dressed and said, "After this plane, things won't be the same," one of my OCD rituals. At the airport, my mom gave me a hug. My dad told me they were proud of me. Then I boarded my one-hour-and-forty-minute flight. Explorers have discovered foreign lands with less preparation.

That night, I met John Wing in the greenroom of Edmonton's Yuk Yuk's. "I'm going to do a chunk about how I hate dieting and working out," he said. "And a lot about the difference between US and Canadian politics."

He was telling me to make sure my jokes didn't stray too close to his. I'd heard opening for another comedian was totally different from doing a regular set in the middle of a warmed-up crowd. You have to be deferential. You can't outshine the headliner. Never run the light and go long. Not even by a minute.

During the first show, I was talking about living with my parents when a guy in a white cowboy hat yelled "loser." I could have lit him up. That hat made him a sitting duck. But I held my tongue. I'd leave him for John to destroy if he heckled again. I avoided crowd work of any kind. If I burned through audience members and John made a similar observation, someone would likely shout out, "He already said that!" A good opener does whatever they can to stack the deck in the headliner's favor.

The next afternoon, John told me to meet him at his hotel. He motioned for me to take a seat and handed me a warm Diet Coke. His laptop played old clips of track-and-field races on YouTube.

"Look at that stride," John said. "That guy on top being one of the quickest off the blocks?"

"Oh, he's great," I said. "Real fast."

When the video concluded, John loaded up another. "Look at this part," he yelled at the screen. "I bet you thought he could over-take him."

It became clear John had seen these races before. I didn't have the acting chops to fake interest, but I settled in for the long haul, worrying this is what I put people through when I talked about the Grateful Dead. The afternoon dragged on as I watched these men whip around the track. Piss him off? Insult him? Do that and I'd never be invited on the road again and would have to go back to ruining Quebecois people's dinners.

On Sunday morning, I boarded a Red Arrow bus whose only open seat was next to the driver, and we departed into a blizzard that would have shut down New York airports, but this was Canada, and we barely shrugged at weather that spelled certain death. The bus chugged along empty fields of white, snow whirling against the windows. We passed signs for Gasoline Alley and Red Deer. I pulled my parka over my knees and read Steve Martin's memoir *Born Standing Up*. On the three-hour trip, I finished eight pages.

———

In Calgary, I crashed on the love seat of one of Pugs's college buddies. He was a teacher and left for school bright and early. With his permission, I slid into his bed and drifted off as my lower half regained circulation. While he was at work, I listened to my sets from the previous weekend and tried to think of tags I could add to my jokes.

On Wednesday, John invited me to lunch. I arrived before him, got us a booth, and started writing something down that I'd thought of on the walk over. I'd gotten into the habit of carrying a digital recorder. I pressed my ear against the speaker, trying to decipher my thoughts. When John arrived, he noticed a Grateful Dead Steal Your Face sticker on my notebook.

"Ah, a keeper of the symbol," he said.

"You're a head!"

"Wow, I've never seen you so elated. Sorry to disappoint you. I like good music. But I did open for Robert Hunter once."

"Are you serious?"

"Yes. Wow, Phil, these energy boosts are really something."

"Where did you open for Hunter?"

"University of Rochester. I had to do an hour. Early show I killed, killed. He goes up and the crowd loves him. He's a great lyricist."

"The best."

"So I walk out for the late show, still on a high from the early, and it's the same crowd. They stayed and they had already heard everything I had."

"What did you do?"

"I tried to do some crowd work."

"Oh, right. You're 'like what you do for a living?' And heads are like . . . 'this.'"

"Ha. I had my guitar there for my closer. Started playing songs."

"How did it go?"

"Good, not great. Until I got to the last song. I figured I'd do an instrumental version of 'Good Lovin'.' I didn't really know the words. Just the chords. I had nothing and . . ."

"The crowd sang along."

"I couldn't believe it. They went crazy. When I came offstage Robert Hunter asked, 'How did you know to play that song?' I played it cool, but I'll tell you, Phil, it was blind luck. Turns out, they played 'Good Lovin'' at every show in the seventies and eighties."

This statement is completely false. The Grateful Dead didn't play "Good Lovin'" every night. Over their thirty-year career, they played it more than four hundred times, which is not as frequent as "Me and My Uncle," which they played over six hundred times. I kept that fact to myself, not wanting John to feel slighted.

"Every night, eh," I said.

"Oh," John said. "I went into the Yuk's office and talked to the booker Rick Graves."

"Isn't he the guy who kicked the pregnant woman?"

"He says she wasn't pregnant. I put a word in for you. Told him you were the Bob Weir of comedy. Expect a call. He's got a bunch of terrible one-nighters in different godforsaken places in Alberta like Lethbridge. Oh, and they don't pay shit."

"Are you serious? Thank you."

"He promised he'd load you up."

I wouldn't be performing in comedy clubs. These gigs were one-nighters in bars and roadhouses in far-flung locations in northern British Columbia and Alberta, the Texas of Canada. No accommodations on off nights. And I'd pay for my travel. Would I come out behind on the gigs? Most likely. Would I stay in quarters that would make the Giusti seem like the Ritz-Carlton? Also yes. But I'd get paid to tell jokes.

My first gig was in Kelowna, BC, opening for Denise Tucker. When I asked if she could drive, she replied, "Not currently."

Driving was not my specialty. A lifelong bonus feature of my dyslexia is poor hand-eye coordination and depth perception. Skills that are very key when it comes to survival behind the wheel. I also knew that when you were an opener, transporting the headliner was often more important than being funny. I picked up the car at 8:30 a.m. to give myself extra time to navigate what might be a treacherous voyage. When I picked up Denise in Chilliwack, I told her I was not a seasoned driver.

"Oh great," she said. "I have chronic neck pain from my last accident."

I put the pieces together and realized why she couldn't drive.

"Hey, do you mind if I smoke pot?" Denise asked. "It's the only thing that helps with the pain."

"I had to sign a thing that said I wouldn't smoke in the car."

"It's only pot."

"I'm really sorry."

She let out a sigh with the lung capacity of someone who never smoked a day in her life. "What if I crack the window?"

I drove on the Trans-Canada Highway, climbing a steep, narrow road into the Canadian Rockies. At the summit pass, the weather turned to whiteout conditions. The lines on the road disappeared. I drove in the middle of the road at a snail's pace, listening to a dissertation on how effective pot was for altitude sickness.

The five-hour trip took eleven. When we pulled into the parking lot of the Blue Line Inn, I got a sinking feeling. Connecting with people who drove monster trucks would be challenging. Inside the bar, men played street hockey in a makeshift rink, shooting pucks into a net. The rest of the clientele looked like they took steroids and only did arms at the gym. They had couch potato beer bellies and fitness fanatic biceps. Those not practicing slap shots watched a UFC fight on a giant screen pulled down over the stage. I found the manager, Jodi, a tiny woman in high-waisted jean shorts and a low-cut tank top.

"You're really late," she told me. "This is the last bout. I'll bring you right up. We've got to keep asses in seats buying drinks."

"Is there a sign or some kind of signal I could give the bouncers if someone's being disruptive?"

"It's Friday night in Kelowna, honey. Everyone is disruptive," Jodi said, chuckling. "Hell, I may heckle you. And I'm the bouncer." I looked around and noticed the all-female staff. Jodi shrugged.

I watched the UFC fight next to a guy who clenched his beer mug so tightly I thought it would shatter. He screamed at the television when one fighter tackled his opponent, flipping him on his back.

"Fuck him up," he yelled.

The fighter obliged, pummeling his opponent's face into a mess of blood. As the referee raised the victor's arm, Jodi nodded at me. I hit the stage before the screen had fully retracted into the ceiling, UFC credits still rolling. Behind me hung the Yuk Yuk's sign covered with dents, likely pummeled with headbutts. The likely culprit, a drunk in hunting fatigues, sat on the edge of the stage. He refused to move.

"I want a good seat," he slurred.

"I'm not starting the show until you move." I immediately regretted my words. I was in a standoff. And I had already almost died once today.

"Be funny," yelled a guy in a Vancouver Canucks jersey.

"The show starts when he gets off the stage," I said.

"Make me laugh and I'll move," said my costar.

A couple in the back, clearly not satisfied with the level of entertainment, got up and walked out. When Jodi saw her customers leaving, she rushed through the tables. Before the guy knew what hit him, she had him in a half nelson and on his feet.

"Jesus, Jod. I was just having some fun."

Instead of throwing him out, she released him into an empty seat in the front row.

"A round of applause for Jodi St-Pierre, everybody," I said. I proceeded to tell thirty minutes of jokes while a drunk hunter who likely had firearms in his monster truck glared at me.

————————

At Christmas, I found myself in a banquet hall in Alberta, standing in a sea of truckers. Their trucking company holiday show was supposed to begin at eight thirty. By ten, the show hadn't started. I ducked into the bathroom. Two truckers went into a stall and made snorting noises.

Three hours after the scheduled showtime, I finally had the mic in hand. I stared out at a room filled with round tables. Round tables are the bane of stand-ups—50 percent of the audience have their backs facing the comic. The half that faced me were also facing their disengaged coworkers. From the stage, I saw that the audience was segregated. Half were coked-up Kid Rock devotees; the other half were Sikh drivers and their families. The only thing that seemed to unite them was their indifference to my comedy.

In the front row, a small childlike man sat with his back to the stage. Every time I tried to tell a joke, he'd pantomime driving a truck. The shouts of his coworkers told me his name was Ricky.

"Ricky," I said. "You've drunk enough that you shouldn't even be pretending to be driving." This got a snicker and made Ricky get up and leave the room.

After a couple jokes, I could feel the show slowly getting on track. Then the door in the back of the room opened to reveal Ricky, standing shirtless.

"Now I got you, motherfucker!" he screamed.

His battle cry was followed by an air raid of tiny tomatoes. Impressively, the flying crudités made it all the way to the stage. None of the mini vegetables made contact, but I'd hit my limit.

"I don't know what's going on with this man," I said. "But he's representing your company. This is unacceptable."

I put the mic on the stool and walked offstage for the first time in my career. The Sikh community gave me a smattering of applause. They might have been happy the show was over, but I like to think they were also sick of Ricky's shit.

A gaggle of truckers followed me out the door. "Come back," they called. "Come back." The crowd parted and Ricky stepped forward, still bare-chested. He looked both sorry and coked up. He stretched out his hand.

"I'm sorry. I'm sorry," he said. "Can we shake hands? Can we shake hands?"

I remembered Ashtray pelting me with toilet paper at the Cobalt. Why did every audience member who threw objects at the stage feel they needed to hug it out? I declined and walked back to my hotel room, where I couldn't wait to make a phone call. There was a new person in my life. Her name was Danielle, and she worked at a soap store in Vancouver and always smelled like a combination of lilac and lavender. She was from the Yukon and considered Vancouver the big city. She lived with her twin sister in a high-rise where they giggled as they spied on their neighbors through high-powered binoculars.

Danielle's pleasant and calming nature was a knee-buckling

contrast to what I sometimes faced performing. I had avoided relationships since I started stand-up, knowing I was less likely to face struggling musicians, squeegee kids, or swingers every night if I had a more pleasant choice. When Danielle and I made plans to hang out when I got home, my anxiety from the terrible gig seemed to dissipate.

My only option, aside from these patchwork one-nighters, was Yuk Yuk's. Comics in Canada have a tolerate/hate relationship with Yuk Yuk's. The franchise has locations all over the country, and they provide a lot of work. But because they have no competition, they set wages. And they set them low. They unite Canadian comics by always giving us something to complain about.

Legend has it that, years ago, a group of Toronto comics protested their wages. The owner, Mark Breslin, who emblazoned his name on every sign hung on every stage, marched to the nearest cemetery, wrote down names from the gravestones, put them on the marquee, and claimed he sold just as many tickets. If that doesn't build a comedy community, nothing will.

Breslin was notorious for insisting that comics sign "Yuk Yuk's exclusive contracts," which prevented us from playing other venues. But if a comic worked Yuk Yuk's clubs every weekend, including Christmas and New Year's Eve, they certainly wouldn't be rich. Nor would they be roommate-less. The conditions were particularly bad for Vancouver comics. Most Yuk Yuk's clubs were around Toronto, and Breslin didn't provide accommodations. We had to sleep on friends' couches.

Frustration built to the point that a summit with Breslin was arranged. Sean Proudlove, a fierce gatekeeper of the Vancouver scene, led the meeting. Proudlove had once threatened to stab a booker in the head with a screwdriver when he refused to pay another comic. A week later the guy had a heart attack. Proudlove took pride in the fact that it had become a cautionary tale for bookers. He once brought a vacuum cleaner onstage to clean up another comic's bomb. A fistfight ensued.

In Vancouver, the comics complained about Yuk Yuk's exclusive contracts. They needed accommodations when they toured through Ontario. Some of them were in their forties with families at home. They were tired of sleeping on futons in disgusting apartments every weekend. After hearing the complaints and not providing any solutions, Breslin concluded the meeting. "Guys, this was great," he said. "And just so you know, I love Vancouver so much. I wanna start spending more time here."

"You can crash on my couch," yelled Proudlove.

Proudlove wasn't booked at Yuk Yuk's again. And nothing changed. Not the shitty contracts. Not the dead-end pay. But Proudlove had humiliated Breslin, which put him in the elite rank of "comic's comic." Someone who likely will never be a household name but will always have a place in the hearts of the few in the know.

For every comedian playing theaters and chopping it up with late-night TV hosts, there are hundreds grinding it out in clubs for scraps. We drive through storms and sleep fully clothed on top of the sheets in hotels where the other clientele are prostitutes and drug addicts. And there are thousands of wannabe comics who would kill for a chance to play those clubs.

I was completely oblivious to these odds. I just kept putting one foot in front of the other, trying to get better. Each hash on my show counter would bring me closer to New York. I visualized being in New York, playing the Comedy Cellar. But I respected the craft so much that I knew I had to earn it. I wouldn't take a shortcut if one was offered. Which worked well, since there's no jumping the line in Canadian comedy. You're not going to get discovered at the Yuk Yuk's in Moncton, New Brunswick. But for the first time in my life, I was doing something that felt like it had potential. Stand-up is a unique skill and the only one I had.

———

My first club tour took me to Toronto. No roadhouses, legion halls, or banquet rooms in chlorine-scented hotels. Just comedy clubs in strip malls in the greater Toronto area. I took a cab from the airport to the lobby of a luxury apartment building at the Harbourfront. A pair of automatic glass doors opened, and there stood a tall figure in navy Hugo Boss slacks and a white dress shirt with the top button undone. An unlit Player's Light cigarette in his mouth. Pugs.

Pugs's apartment had a view of the CN Tower and a flat-screen television that cost more than all my possessions combined. After university, he'd gotten a job writing code for IBM. He showed me his spare bedroom, which fit a queen bed.

"This is Phil's room," he said.

"You're fucking right it is. This is sweet, Pugs."

I stayed with Pugs for months at a time, whenever I could string together back-to-back weekends in Ontario. I took on the role of househusband, cooking healthy dinners and encouraging him to decorate. He still used a stepladder as a nightstand. No matter how long I stayed, he never took a penny of rent. Best of all, Pugs had a car, which I borrowed for gigs. He didn't get angry when I misread a sign and filled his diesel car with regular gas. He's just that Canadian.

One evening, Pugs and I were smoking Lebanese hash when the Yuk Yuk's booker phoned with an offer for a private show. "It's a seventieth birthday party," she said. "We don't offer these privates to everybody. I'll give you the details." I quickly handed the phone to Pugs. Hash was not going to help my already poor ability to write down details.

The following Saturday, we headed for a tiny town outside of Kitchener, Ontario. Pugs claimed his presence wasn't because of the gas incident, but I had my suspicions. We drove down a country road, stopping in front of a ramshackle house with peeling paint.

"This can't be right," I said.

"It's the address," Pugs said.

"What do I do?"

"You go tell your jokes in a crack house."

"Pull up to the street behind the house," I said. "I don't want you catching a glimpse of this. This is as close to prostitution as it comes."

"You are inching closer."

The front door was open, so I knocked on the screen. An elderly woman holding a beer appeared and said, "You must be the professional comedian."

If only, I thought.

"I'm Debra, come on in. Oh wait, do you need to get your equipment?" she asked. "It's Dennis's big night. He's going to be thrilled."

I followed her through the house. She paused in the kitchen. "I think you can just wait in here and I'll introduce you."

"Sounds good," I lied.

"Okie dokie," she said. "Oh. What name do you go by?"

Equipment? An alias? Debra was freaking me out. What were they anticipating?

I waited in the kitchen for my cue. When Debra called my name, I walked out onto a back porch where five old men sat in lawn chairs, sipping beer. No microphone. No lights. No pride. Out in the street, Pugs was parked right in my line of vision. I could see him panicking, deciding what to do. He settled on reclining his seat and disappearing from view.

Dennis and the boys smiled at me, so I went into my act. The most surreal part was that I did really well. Even crowd work was hitting. After forty-five minutes, I said, "Dennis, I was honored to celebrate your birthday with you," and walked down the stairs, out the gate, and into Pugs's car.

"Let's get out of here," I said.

"No shit. Daddy needs a cigarette. How was it? I kept thinking you were going to burn your head on that bug light."

"There was a bug light?"

That was my one and only back porch performance. I would have done more. In school, I tried and failed to avoid adversity. With stand-up, I leaned into it. Every chance I got I went into situations that, on paper, were the last place anyone would want to perform.

Every time I survived, I thought of how easy it would be to entertain people who actually wanted to hear comedy. People who had bought tickets. People willing to leave their back porch.

The more I sacrificed for comedy, the mightier I became. School had prepared me for struggle. I was programmed to expect adversity and to assume life would be hard. My friends outside of comedy were buying houses, raising kids, and putting money away for retirement. In a way, I pitied them. I got to work each day at something I loved. Telling jokes was its own reward.

When I returned from Toronto, Nathan came to see me headline at the Comedy Mix, formerly the Yuk Yuk's where I'd performed on Crash and Burn nights. I improvised with the crowd for long stretches of my set. "During those riffs in between jokes you are completely yourself," Nathan said after the show. "I've never seen anyone use material merely as a jumping-off point."

It was the greatest compliment I'd ever received, because the Grateful Dead used their songs simply as starting points. They never played the same show twice. They would cycle through their massive catalog, playing with the order of the set list, seeing what new elements they could find in the songs or between the songs. The crowd always wondered what was going to happen next. Unpredictability is also what makes a joke funny. I had the idea to apply that technique to my whole show, not just the individual jokes. One night at Yuk Yuk's Toronto, I picked out an older guy near the stage and asked if he was dyslexic.

"I think I am," he said.

"Well, they can tell in first grade," I said. "I'm sorry nobody told you."

I'd established a "character" in the audience. Later in the set, I could return to the undiagnosed dyslexic and play off him for laughs. Then I asked if there were any teachers in the audience. There was always at least one.

"What do you teach?" I asked.

"First grade."

"Can you tell if a child is dyslexic at that age?"

"Absolutely."

"Really? 'Cause this guy is like fifty and he's struggling," I said. "He just tried to put ketchup in his gin and tonic."

As a set got rolling, I would create a "cast" of audience members. I'd pop over to the teacher, then back to the dyslexic. Each new inter-action functioned like a spontaneous riff in a song. If every one of my shows felt different, people might come see me twice. And every night, performing felt fresh to me as well. If I could find a new beat in my act, discover a new way to interact with the crowd, crashing on couches and seventy-five-dollar paychecks didn't bother me. I could endure anything. I knew it was all leading somewhere. Epic bus journeys, hazardous motel rooms, and nightly drunken heck-lers were rites of passage. They all brought me closer to my goal of performing stand-up in New York City.

12

Pain + Time Equals Comedy

At Montreal's Just For Laughs, Corey ran his sound check to five hundred empty seats. We'd both landed spots on the Homegrown competition at the biggest comedy festival in the world. Only the winner and the runner-up stayed for the rest of the festival. The other eight comics had to be out of the hotel by the next morning.

Corey had the archetype factor going for him—he was heavyset, with longish hair and a gruff voice. Pothead Jack Black. He glided through the comedy world with ease, the way the other students had breezed through school. He'd started comedy years after me and was already at JFL and had appeared on television. I performed anywhere that happened to have a microphone. Although I made exceptions.

"I've been running the shit out of my set," I told Corey after sound check. "I hope it's ready."

"Really?" he asked. "I haven't done stand-up in three weeks."

Corey reminded me of my high school classmates bragging that they hadn't studied before finals. I resent people who take success for granted and feel a deep kinship with those who struggle.

Those are my people. Dyslexia demands that when I read, write, organize, plan, or differentiate my right hand from my left, I concentrate with all my attention. I marvel when I see people walking down the street texting. Cocky motherfuckers. It's as impressive as parallel parking a fire truck.

Stand-up required the same intense focus. The idea of taking three weeks off before a major festival was as ludicrous as me getting a job as a courtroom stenographer. Jerry Seinfeld said he'd run a set two hundred times before it was ready for *The Tonight Show*. His goal was to not skip a beat even if someone slapped him in the face. I took Seinfeld's words as gospel and had labored over my seven-minute set for months.

I had to kill tonight. I'd tried out for JFL six times. The last year, I'd showcased in front of the festival's booker. Patty, who'd had a few drinks, was infuriated when I wasn't picked. "This is bullshit. You were the funniest," she insisted, charging backstage. "I'm going to give that bald fuck a piece of my mind."

I formed a human blockade and pleaded, "I need that guy to like me." I was devastated that I had to wait another year before trying again. Despite the annual rejection, I thought, I dare you to try and deny me next year.

Getting JFL was crucial. I would get a valuable letter of recommendation for my American O-1 work visa. My immigration lawyer suggested I get as many as possible. And it was my first chance to stand out. No one has ever gotten scouted in Williams Lake, British Columbia.

At Cinquième Salle, the house lights went down over a sold-out crowd. Corey snuck a look from behind the curtain at row after row of industry figures who had the power to put comics on television in America. For Canadian comics, TV spots in the States were rare. A way out of never-ending Yuk Yuk's in mini-malls.

"Oh shit," Corey said. "Now I'm nervous."

"Maybe you should have taken six weeks off," I suggested.

When my turn came, I walked out into the lights and faced the crowd. I opened with my stay-at-home son material and then moved into my dyslexia chunk. "I was in special ed," I said. "My mom did all my homework, all my projects, and they still put me in special ed. My sweet mom would always say to me, 'There's nothing to be ashamed of, being in special ed.' I'm glad she felt that way. Technically she was in it too. If your mom does your homework, parent-teacher conferences are a very different vibe. Because the teacher would say, 'Phil needs to put in more effort,' and my mom would say, 'How dare you! He's working full-time and raising three kids.'"

I took runner-up. Corey took the next flight out of Montreal. The winner performed what I'll politely call a bad Dane Cook homage. He accented his every-douche observations by humping the stool, an alarmingly common practice at the time. I felt an impulse to take the stool humpers of the world aside and ask, "Have you ever observed anything about the world besides how women dance at the club?"

The next day, I picked up a copy of the *Hollywood Reporter* and saw they'd printed one of my jokes: "I've been told when you meet the right person, you know immediately. How come when you meet the wrong person, it takes a year and a half?" I saved the press clipping for my O-1 file.

For the next three days, I performed at eight shows around Montreal. At JFL after-parties, I shook hands with agents and managers and pretended to read their business cards. At a hotel bar, a guy with horn-rimmed glasses and a salt-and-pepper beard told me my clean material could work on television. His name was Bart Coleman, and he was a segment producer for *The Late Late Show* with Craig Ferguson.

"I caught your set the other night. We'd love to have you on the show," Coleman said. Then he asked the question Canadian comics hate to hear: "What's your immigration status?"

"I'm in the process of getting my O-1. A letter from you would really help." I'd never been so direct.

"Absolutely. Here's my card. I expect to hear from you."

———

I'd aspired to live in America since I was a kid. As a teenager, I hid my stash in the inseam of my boxers, knowing if the Oshawa cops found it, they would end my American dream. The moment my parents dropped me off on Shalom's doorstep, I vowed to find a way to work legally in New York. Modeling hadn't panned out. And American comedy clubs wouldn't book a Canadian without a visa. One Vancouver comedian had been stopped at the border. A customs officer Googled his name and discovered he'd plugged a New York show on his website. Banned from entering the United States, he quit comedy and got a job working for Xbox. Game over.

Back in Vancouver, I sent Bart Coleman the template for a "support letter." An O-1 visa required proof that I was an "Individual with Extraordinary Ability or Achievement." The phrase "Rising Star" was a no go. Uncle Sam wanted people who had already ascended. I also sent Bart stand-up sets I'd filmed with a digital camcorder. Bart told me he was a massive Deadhead. We are everywhere.

With Bart's support letter in hand, I faced what I had been dreading. With a sigh, I sat down at the kitchen table. The unreadable stack of visa forms drained my life force. My mom set down her tea on a place mat and assured me, "It won't take long, dear. Let's get it over with."

"I should have stayed in Oshawa and lived out my years," I said dramatically.

"And you would have been terribly unhappy. Come on, Delphi, I have to make dinner. Your sister will be here soon."

Then my mom did something she'd done since I was a kid. She used a bookmark to highlight what she was reading line by line. My mom didn't need a bookmark to follow along. She was a voracious reader who tackled dense prose with no hands. But she knew the technique helped me. She normalized it. Whenever I messed up a simple line item or checked the wrong box, my mom fixed it and tried to search for an unrelated compliment. One I never let her forget was when, out of nowhere, she reminded me that I looked good in my navy-blue suit. We were on the last form when Patty buzzed up.

"Are you helping Phil with his homework again?" Patty asked.

Patty was pregnant. Our family was filled with the excitement of a sports team about to draft an all-star recruit. We were in a losing slump after my nervous breakdown and with my dad struggling to adjust to retirement. He had taken to checking the stock market incessantly and swearing at what he saw. That night, my mom and I dropped the thick manila envelope in the mailbox.

"You must feel relieved, dear," my mom said.

"I will when it gets approved."

"Don't be silly. Of course it will. Just wait a little longer."

I was used to waiting. Waiting for the school bell to ring so I could be relieved from my excruciating boredom. Waiting to be old enough to get the fuck out of Oshawa. Waiting to discover what I was good at. Waiting for intrusive thoughts to vacate my brain. Waiting for Zoloft to work. Waiting for Wellbutrin to leave my system. Waiting in disgusting motel rooms for showtime. Waiting for New York. Waiting, as Jerry sang, for a miracle.

Waiting meant gigs in towns like Cranbrook, a redneck hamlet at the base of the Canadian Rockies. On a Saturday night just before Christmas, I descended into the basement of the Kootenay Country Inn. A manager wearing a camouflage parka showed me a vinyl dance floor lined with booths.

"Do not stick around after your set," the manager advised. "The venue turns into a nightclub. Comics keep getting beaten up."

"But the show is safe, right?" I asked.

"We haven't had a problem in months."

Come showtime, the club didn't bother to set up chairs in front of the stage. The audience hunched in the booths, so far away I couldn't make out their shapes in the dark. I bombed into the abyss.

Back at my hotel, I sat fully clothed on the bed, calculating how many hours until my flight home. A stench permeated my room. I wrote my concerns off as OCD, but when the other comic stopped by, he said what I had been thinking: "Your room smells like meat."

I found the night clerk at the front desk reading the pamphlet about the hotel. "Hi," I said. "My room smells like meat."

"It shouldn't," he said in a tone that suggested, "410 hasn't had a deli counter in years." He refused to switch me, but I was happy we were on the same page.

Back in Vancouver, Danielle picked me up from the airport and we rushed to St. Paul's Hospital. Patty had given birth while I was in the air. In the hospital room, I was met by my parents' beaming faces. I darted to Patty's bedside. She cradled Marty. She'd named him after my dad.

"Have a seat, and you can hold him," Patty said.

When Patty handed over Marty, he wiggled to be closer to me. I had a new favorite person. I hoped Jerry would understand.

"Why are you holding him so high?" Patty asked. "He's not a rotary telephone."

"I wanted to take him in," I said.

I held Marty to my chest and prayed that he wasn't dyslexic. "Please let this Hanley have a smooth ride," I begged the universe. "No Learning Resource Centers or short buses. No ridicule. No OCD. No bullshit for this one, please. May spell-check always understand what he's going for."

I had just finished my morning meditation when my mom shouted, "Delphi, come up here, please. I think this is it."

I took the stairs two at a time. I opened the envelope and handed it back to her, not trusting my reading ability.

"You got it!" she shouted as her feet left the ground.

My dad said we better drive down to the border first thing in the morning. "Phil, I'm serious," he huffed. "The train pulls out of the station at nine."

"He has plenty of time, Martin," my mom said.

"Who knows what the hell will happen? The market is in the dumper."

The US Department of Labor was a concrete-colored building just over the Canadian border. I waited in line with my mom in case they sprang any last-minute forms on me. Confirmation letter and passport in hand, I approached the counter. A giant man with biceps on the brink of bursting through the sleeves of his blue uniform stapled a card into my passport, entered the date, and hit it with a large rubber stamp. He came around the counter.

"Are you the mother?" he asked.

"I certainly am," said my mom, beaming.

He reached out his mammoth hand to me. "Welcome to America."

After eight years of struggle, I'd done it. Finally, I could work in New York. Accomplishment felt unfamiliar. Dyslexia never prevented me from setting goals, but it certainly had stopped me from achieving them. Not this time.

My dad and Danielle applauded when we got back in the car.

"Delphi is going to wake in a city that never sleeps," sang my dad. He had dreamed of living in the States and attempted to make the move when my parents first got married, but then was told he'd be drafted and sent to Vietnam. Staying in Oshawa won by a nose.

On the drive back to Canada, I stared out the window, remembering the night I'd sat on my back porch in Oshawa and my parents had told me college wasn't a good idea. The night I accepted my education was over. The night I realized I had to take a very different path from the ones my friends and family had followed. But I'd walked it, and it was worth it. My mom framed a copy of my visa and hung it on the wall next to my sister's diploma. Just as Patty had earned the right to work in her field, I could now work in mine.

———

Work might be a bit of a stretch. On a Sunday night, I walked through the East Village, passing the Indian restaurant where Shalom had convinced me to try modeling. I ducked into a restaurant called Three of Cups on the next corner. The server seemed surprised to see a customer.

"Is there a comedy show here?" I asked.

"Downstairs," she said, deflated.

At the bottom of the rickety stairs was a room filled with forty folding chairs. Three were occupied. Onstage, a comedian talked about a homeless guy on the subway. That's going to murder in the Midwest, I thought. Leaning against the bar stood a short guy with glasses, his hair styled like a toupee.

"I'm looking for someone named T.J.," I said.

"J.T., 'tis I."

"Oh hey, I'm Phil. Aubrey told me that he spoke to you about me doing a spot sometime."

"Send a tape," he said, turning his back.

I was starting from scratch. Again. I couldn't get on bottom-of-the-barrel open mics. No one cared that I was a headliner in Canada or that I'd played Just For Laughs. All I could do was show up at every shitty bar show and club in the city and ask (or beg) for unpaid spots.

I visited New York for monthlong stints, adding to my long list of roommates and my desire to someday live on my own. I hustled to get myself known before I'd have to return to Canada for paid work. I constantly traveled back and forth between Vancouver and New York City. It wasn't just the miles; it was the relationships. On the one side, I had Marty and my family in Vancouver. And I was deeply in love with Danielle. On the other side was New York, where my comedic future would be determined. For a year and a half, I struggled to live two lives and tried to decide which one to focus on.

––––––

In March, I walked through the black gates of CBS Television City on Beverly Boulevard in Hollywood. In my suit bag, I had a bottle-green cashmere cardigan Ronnie had mailed me when he found out I was going to be on television. I suspected he'd bought it new, although he denied it vehemently. "Retail cashmere?" he said when I called to thank him. "Phylicia, what are you on about?"

I made my way through the lots to Studio 56. *The Late Late Show*'s set was smaller than it looked on TV. Bart Coleman brought me to hair and makeup and asked, "So what do you want to plug?"

"I got nothing. Except a weekend opening for someone at Go Bananas in Cincinnati."

On a monitor in the greenroom, I watched Craig Ferguson teach Amanda Peet to play harmonica. "Just stick it in your mouth and blow," Ferguson told her. After she exited to wild applause, Ferguson couldn't get out my plug for Go Bananas without cracking up.

"How dare you?" quipped Geoff, his animatronic skeleton cohost.

"Why the hell can't I play Go Bananas?" Ferguson riffed. "Why am I stuck here at CBS?" He manipulated a monkey doll like a ventriloquist's puppet. "Go Bananas," said the monkey. "I'm there!"

Then Ferguson ended the show and walked off. "They'll change the set, then you go on," Bart told me. "It looks seamless in post."

When the "On Air" sign switched off, Ferguson appeared in the hallway. "Thanks for doing the show," he said, not breaking his stride. Disappearing out an exit, he looked over his shoulder and shouted, "Don't fuck up."

Not exactly Johnny Carson inviting Seinfeld to the couch.

"He has a newborn at home," Bart explained.

Bart led me out into the wings of the studio. A line producer shut the soundproof door behind us. I fidgeted with the buttons of my cardigan. "I was listening to the first Dead show I ever went to," Bart said, placing a hand on my shoulder.

"My first show was the greatest night of my life. What was your first show?" I asked.

"Boston. October 21, '91."

"Oh man, I love those Hornsby runs. That New Minglewood is nasty."

Bart shook his head and smiled like he was reliving it.

"The second set pre-drums was amazing. Cumberland, Saint, Eyes," I said.

Bart held up a finger, listening to his headset. "You're on in thirty seconds," he said calmly. "But what really blew my mind was seeing JGB."

"You saw Jerry Band?"

"Nine times," Bart said and gave me a gentle push. I stepped out of the wings, hit my mark, looked at the camera, and said, "I'm not only a comedian, I'm also a stay-at-home son."

After a few jokes landed, I realized what Bart had done. Discussing the Dead had made me as relaxed and calm as I could be given the circumstances. Once again, Jerry saved the day.

———

Kevin Brennan walked into the greenroom of Go Bananas in Cincinnati and tossed a water bottle in the wastebasket. Brennan had started stand-up in Chicago, then moved to New York, where he worked for *Saturday Night Live* in the late '90s, writing Weekend Update segments with Colin Quinn. He'd been a regular at the Comedy Cellar for twenty-five years.

"You killed," I said.

"Gee, thanks," he quipped sarcastically. "Estee would love your act."

I knew about Estee, the legendary booker at the Comedy Cellar. She'd been at the helm since the '80s, guiding its transformation from a music venue to a struggling comedy club to the most revered stand-up venue on the planet.

"That capri joke. She'll love you," Brennan continued. "I'll call her tomorrow and get you an audition. I'm batting a hundred percent for people I've vouched for. No pressure."

"I'm not ready for that."

"Not ready?"

"Well, I'm on the road a bunch the next little bit."

"Do it when you'll be around New York for a while. Let me know. I'll make the call."

Back at my hotel, I Skyped Danielle. She had installed the app on my laptop on her only visit to New York. What would have been an all-day affair for me, struggling with simple written instructions, she'd done in three minutes. As with all my partners, I'd come to rely on Danielle for day-to-day tasks. She'd become my IT guy and had been recently promoted to my travel agent.

"You look pretty," I said.

"Thank you. See, I told you Skype was easy. Isn't this better? We can see each other."

"I hate the word. I can't spell it. The *e* bugs me."

"How was the weekend?"

"Kevin Brennan said he'd vouch for me at the Comedy Cellar," I said.

"Yay! Oh God, when?"

"I lied and said I'm out of town. I want to wait till I'm ready. New York crowds are different. I want to get comfortable and really blow her away."

"You killed on TV."

"This is bigger."

―――――――

Back in Vancouver, I arrived at Toys "R" Us as it was closing. The teenage cashier was clearly thrown by my luggage. "Just checking in," I said. It didn't bomb so much as baffle. "I'm joking," I said. "But can I leave my stuff here? I'll be right back."

"We close in two-point-five minutes."

"Thank you," I shouted over my shoulder as I cleared off the Play-Doh shelf.

After a late-night stroll with my luggage, I knocked on Patty's door. She appeared unfazed with Marty on her hip.

"I'm sorry it's so late. My flight in Minneapolis was delayed," I said.

"Minneapolis?"

"Stopover."

"Marty, look who it is."

"Dil." Marty smiled and reached for me. I gathered him in my arms, and he pointed to the bedroom. "Bed Dil," he said, indicating he wanted to play with his stuffed animals. He meant business.

"First, I got something for you."

I put Marty in his high chair and pulled out the containers of

Play-Doh one at a time. He kicked his feet and clapped his perfect little hands. "Ooooooooooo," he said in disbelief.

By the time the Play-Doh had been mixed into a soccer ball of brown, I was back in New York.

———————

That November, after months on the road, working in New York, and barely seeing my girlfriend, Danielle picked me up at Erik Nielsen International Airport. It was seven degrees Fahrenheit in Whitehorse.

"Welcome to the Yukon," she said, squeezing me tight.

"God, I missed you."

We got into her dad's giant GMC truck. It was surreal to see her at the wheel of this beast. "We have to go to the store to get supplies. There's a storm coming," she said, checking her mirrors.

"Supplies? Why are you talking like a prospector?"

"Maybe I am now."

The Real Canadian Superstore had an apocalyptic vibe. People speed walked up and down the aisles, grabbing what was left on the shelves. I admired their hustle. New York had taught me to appreciate people who choose to live in harsh environments. Of course, New York's inconveniences are man-made, and the Yukon's are because Mother Nature hates them.

"I thought this was our least-populated province," I said. "Why so busy?"

"We're the second least," said Danielle. "It's the storm."

When we pulled up to her parents' house at 5 p.m., the sun had already set. The Yukon is such a hard place to live that the Canadian government has offered significant amounts of cash to anyone willing to relocate and raise a family there. Danielle's family had taken the government up on their offer and now owned a giant house with a hot tub that provided a view of the stars year-round.

After a couple days, Danielle and I drove to a cabin just over the border in Alaska and found the only dive bar in Skagway. It was lit as brightly as an operating room, I assumed to compensate for the months of darkness. We were approached by a drunk couple in their forties.

"Where are you two from?" slurred the woman.

I pretended not to hear her and announced, "It's so good to be home."

"You're not from here," she insisted.

"What do you mean? We know each other. I thought quite well if I'm being honest."

"Poppycock. What's my name then?"

"What's my nickname for you, do you mean?"

Danielle giggled.

"Go on."

"Delicate flower."

The lady smiled, exposing her red-wine teeth, and grabbed my arm. "I like you."

"Let me get you a drink," I said. "One red wine for DF."

"How did you know that's what I drink? My grandfather was Italian."

"Nonno."

"How do you know that? You're freaking me out."

"You're so funny," said Danielle.

"Thank you," I said, taken aback.

"I guess I never get to see that side of you," she said and kissed me on the cheek.

I got a sick feeling. Our whole relationship I had been chasing stand-up. Catching a flight to the next city. The next gig. Running back to New York. Sleeping in shitty hotels instead of in bed next to my girlfriend. I told myself I'd someday make up for lost time, but I'd been saving the best part of myself for strangers who bought a two-drink minimum. Despite the endless hours I spent meditating, when it came to our relationship I was not in the moment.

The next morning, extremely hungover, I put the Grateful Dead on the truck's stereo for the drive back to Canada. "Not again," Danielle said, switching the music to The National. In five years, Danielle hadn't once complained about the Dead. I considered them the soundtrack of our relationship. I felt guilty. So guilty that I didn't mention that The National were Deadheads.

That night, Danielle was silent as she got ready for bed. I didn't ask what was wrong, hoping she was just sad I had to leave for New York the next morning. In bed, I spooned her. Her cold feet made me wince.

"Good night. I love you," I said.

"Enough to move to the Yukon?" she asked.

I didn't answer and rolled over on my back. Once Danielle was asleep, I got up to use the bathroom. Out the window shone the aurora borealis. Green and purple light flickered over the snow-covered ground. High school acid Phil would have really loved this, I thought. Then it dawned on me that I had never done acid with my high school girlfriend. I wasn't funny with Danielle and had never tripped with my first love. What stopped me from sharing my passions?

———————

A month later, I was performing at a Christmas party in Regina, Canada. Yes, one of the major cities in Canada is called Regina (ri-jahy-nuh). Canadians are simply mature enough to handle it. The gig was for regional employees of KFC. Everyone in the audience looked like Eminem, at a time when Eminem no longer looked like Eminem.

The moment I grabbed the mic, I looked into the crowd and saw zero sign of Christmas cheer. Just three minutes into my contractual forty-five-minute set, during a tried-and-true bit that went "I had a huge problem with high school bullies . . . on my way to the show tonight," a guy in the front yelled, "Pussy jokes!" To his credit, it received the first laugh of the night. The evening quickly devolved into drunken men shouting at me as I struggled through my set, resulting in the biggest bomb of my career.

I couldn't get into the elevator fast enough. To my horror, as I frantically pushed the close button, it filled with people from the party. I shrank into the corner, trying to will myself invisible.

"What did you think of the comedian?" one guy asked another.

"What comedian?" his friend replied.

Finally back in my room, desperate for some comfort, I called

213

Danielle. Despite the last night of our trip, we'd had a great month. I had been more attentive. I was particularly excited because we were making final arrangements for the next day. I was set to fly back to Vancouver. She was also returning there, from her parents' place in Yukon. Our flights were aligned to land within minutes of each other, so my dad could retrieve us at the same time. I was so excited to see her that I expected to barely sleep that night.

As soon as she answered the phone, I knew something was wrong.

"Is everything okay?" I asked.

She began to cry, heaving loud sobs into the phone.

"I think we should break up," she finally said. "I'm not coming tomorrow."

Between crying fits, she told me it was the hardest thing she'd ever done and explained that she'd decided to stay in the Yukon.

I'd been dumped before. It hurts no matter what the circumstances are, but to be dumped for the Yukon? That's a monumental kind of pain. To be told that the least habitable part of Canada is more appealing than you? Ouch. Somehow, this desolate, harsh tundra, a place where kids don't understand Annie's song "Tomorrow" because the sun doesn't rise for weeks, was easier to contend with than dating me.

I returned to Vancouver, professionally and personally devastated. I was too heartbroken to eat, and to make matters worse, because it was Christmas there were no shows. With nothing to distract me, I retreated to my room. All I could think about was our last conversation, and I began to write "I think we should break up" over and over again, as a freewriting exercise. I was looking for a way out of this pain. Then, at my saddest, loneliest moment, I found it. I wrote what I wished I had said in reply: "Sorry, I didn't hear that. I think the phone cut out, but I think we should break up."

Suddenly the pain was flipped. I continued to improvise this alternate history, one in which I broke up with Danielle, to her dismay. In fifteen minutes, I completed an original and uniquely funny bit, something that would normally take months and months to fine-tune. I quickly drafted a short script of this make-believe conversation, and the first time I performed it, I invited a woman onstage to play the role of the girlfriend.

"This is so hard," the woman read, trying to stifle her laughter. "You're such a great guy and I love that you still live with your parents. I can't believe I won't get the chance to make love to you tonight. That is something I highly recommend to any single woman or someone who is in a relationship."

"Sorry, the phone cut out again. What was that last part?"

"I was just saying that every woman on the planet should get to experience the forbidden pleasure that only you can provide."

"True dat."

I continued: "All right, babe, wish you the best."

"I've already had the best. I'll always love you, Donkey Hammer."

The bit killed. It was five solid minutes of laughter. I'd go on to perform that piece hundreds of times, always with a random guest from the audience, in packed theaters and at comedy festivals. I even did it on television, taking the risk of performing alongside an audience member with the cameras rolling. Audiences ate it up.

They loved watching me enact the fantasy we all have of wishing we could revise tragic moments. Bringing a stranger onstage added another level of tension and release, especially as she'd read her lines about what a great lover I was and how much she'd miss it, further embellishing my fantasy.

It was also a departure from my earlier work. It blended my improv background, my general good looks that had made my modeling career, and my stand-up delivery. More than comedy, it taught me I could make anything funny, and I realized the more painful the event, the more potential I had to create laughter.

Recently, while I was hanging out with a bunch of other comedians, one mentioned that his father had died of alcoholism when he was ten. Another comic, someone very well established, immediately quipped, "Now that'll make you funny."

It's true that in comedy, your tears create laughter for others. By quickly perusing Richard Pryor's Wikipedia page, you'll find this is not a new thing. Pryor, considered by many to be the greatest of all time, faced adversity and tragedy from the get-go. I can say unequivocally: I would not be a comedian if I hadn't been dyslexic and mistreated by the school system. I once had a therapist describe my ability to take my struggles in school and turn them into material as "the wound and the bow." Taking a weakness and making a strength.

Thankfully the tragedy doesn't always need to be monumental. Something as common as a dysfunctional relationship can produce great jokes. It is my favorite aspect of comedy that no matter how painful a situation, there is always a bright side. You're going to get material. Getting a solid bit from a traumatic event makes me feel like Rumpelstiltskin.

Without the relationship, without that reason to stay around Vancouver, and with a newfound confidence, I decided to make the move to New York. All it took was a broken heart.

———

But I never booked my flight. I'd open my laptop, pull up Expedia .com, then slam the screen down. It wasn't my dyslexia stopping me; it was the thought of leaving Marty. I remained in stasis until I confessed my feelings to my mom.

"I shouldn't leave now," I told her. "Marty is going to start walking soon. I don't want to miss that."

"Delphi, we didn't spend months on your visa paperwork for nothing," my mom said.

"I need to be here for Marty."

"Phil, that's not an uncle's role," my mom said. "You can't sacrifice your career for your nephew. Marty needs you to go. Isn't it better if he has an uncle to look up to, who followed his dreams?"

"But . . . I just . . ."

"Come on, dear, I'll help you book the flight," my mom said. "Make sure we get the date right."

The day before my departure, Patty took Marty into the bathroom and cut a lock of his hair. I sealed it in a tiny plastic bag, put it in my pocket, and recited a Grateful Dead lyric: "I will not forgive you, if you will not take the chance." Then I moved to New York. I hoped for the last time.

13

Out of This World

By the time I moved to New York, I'd had thirty-seven roommates. Thirty-nine if you include my parents. Numbers forty and forty-one were a DJ and an actress, two professions that can attract dicey personalities. After the Mrs. O'Connor saga back in England, I just hoped they weren't religious fanatics. But with two cats each and "coparenting" a pit bull, there was evidence they were building an ark.

At a luxury apartment building in Williamsburg, I picked up keys from the doorman and took the elevator to the seventh floor. I was unlocking my door when I saw a familiar pair of cheekbones strutting down the hallway.

"Phil," called Jason Drydon. "Did we meet in Düsseldorf?"

"Jason, holy shit."

"Wait, did you buy this place?" he asked. "I didn't know it was on the market. We bought ours last year. We're going to be neighbors."

I pictured handing a real estate agent the mountain of drink tickets I'd earned since I quit modeling.

"The gig we did in Germany was my last modeling job," I said.

"I stuck with it, for better or worse," Jason said, pulling his keys out of his pocket. A Brazilian woman wearing very little clothing appeared in his doorway.

"Babe, this is Phil," Jason said. "We modeled together. Long time ago."

We exchanged smiles. Then her tone changed. "Jason, you're late for yoga," she said. "Kate is already here."

"Couples yoga," said Jason, rolling his eyes. "Dude, let's get lunch. I mean it."

"Sounds good."

I didn't mean it.

As my new pit bull roommate Dutch welcomed me energetically, I questioned my decision to quit modeling. Why hadn't my parents talked me out of it? I'd found a career where reading wasn't required and that didn't involve a shovel or fulfilling sexual requests, and they encouraged me to see what else was out there. You know, take the temperature of the job market for someone without the ability to compose a résumé. Who is going to hire someone who can't even apply?

That night, I caught the L to an East Village bar that resembled the Korova Milk Bar from *A Clockwork Orange*. A guy with a maniacal laugh raced around the sparse audience, force-feeding them free Jell-O shots while 1980s aerobics videos were projected onto the stage. Sam Morril, a tall comedian with a deep voice, told jokes with a woman's spandex camel toe flickering across his face. Sam had strong setup/punch line jokes drawn from his life. Comedy the way I liked it.

The next day, I bumped into Sam on the corner outside of my new apartment. He lived across the street in an old factory that had been converted into apartments. He could only put a rough estimate on the number of his roommates but confirmed that the lunatic with the Jell-O shots was one of them. The rest were Japanese exchange students.

Sam had grown up in New York City. He'd known he wanted to be a comedian since he was a kid. Like me, Sam was a class clown. Unlike me, he could read. I'd made smart-ass remarks in class because I was bored and angry; Sam was in it for the love of the game. Soon we were meeting every morning at the crack of noon. We bounced bits as we walked to Cafe Colette for lattes. Sam complained that the drip coffee from New York diners was cheaper, but acquiesced because he said the pretentious coffee suited my pretentious clothes.

In the evenings, we met on the same corner and rode the subway into Manhattan, dismantling our jokes like old cars and examining their parts. Sam and I had kindred comedic instincts, obsessed with concise wording and punch lines that stood on their own, no simulated sex with the stool required. In the city, we did shows in bars where the stage was often so close to the bartender I could hear the patrons' orders. If someone's drink required a shaker, there would be a hole in my set.

The place to be seen was Kabin in the East Village. One night, I leaned against the bar, trying to look approachable. A comedy show was happening in the back room, and comics packed the front bar. Everyone seemed to know each other. New York comics were obsessed with pro wrestling and drinking, two things I hadn't been passionate about since I was a kid.

I'd been nursing my Sierra Nevada so long that it was warm and putrid. I gave myself a time limit to socialize. I would force myself to endure that period, like an ice bath or a conversation about someone's cat. Then I was free to go home and have a conversation about a cat. If an out-of-shape guy with a beard ordered a beer, I could safely assume he was a comedian.

"You going up tonight?" I asked a schlubby guy in a flannel.

"Nah, I was on two weeks ago."

"It's wild how long you have to wait to get up here," I said. "It's not like that in Canada."

"Did you work for Yuk Yuk's?" the work-hungry comic asked.

"All over the country."

"Who books that?"

"Who books that?" is the "What's your sign?" of the comedy world. Networking at this subterranean level didn't feel like a step forward; it was a reminder of how very far there was to go.

"It all goes through the main office in Toronto," I replied. My evasive answer was the "not tonight I have a headache" of the comedy world.

"I got to get up early," he said, realizing he wasn't getting any tonight.

"Morning writing session?"

"Dog walking."

I was so desperate to connect in the hopes of making a friend that I watched the Kentucky Derby with open mic-ers and caught a midnight showing of *The Expendables*. Dutch the pit bull became a trusted confidant. The DJ and the actress always said they wanted to come to a show, but I feared that if they saw where I was performing, they'd assume I couldn't cover rent.

Every morning, I looked forward to meeting Sam for coffee. One day, he told me he had an audition at the Comedy Cellar. Just knowing someone about to audition gave me anxiety. Legend had it that you only got one chance to impress Estee. If your set didn't go well, you had to wait five years before you could try out again.

The next morning, I saw Sam waiting on our corner. "Dude, how did it go?" I shouted. "I texted you last night."

"Sorry, I thought I replied. I got passed."

"Congratulations! I knew you would. How do you feel?"

"Hungover."

The next week, Sam went out for lunch with Gary Gulman. Instead of feeling jealous like I had when Pugs had gone off to college, when Sam got passed at the Cellar I felt one step closer to that goal. For the first time in my life, envy was tempered with optimism.

The next night Sam and I bumped into each other at a hostel show in Chelsea. "I'm going to the Cellar to hang," Sam told me. "Come with. We can head home together."

"Thanks, but I'm good for now," I said.

When I finally went through the Cellar's doors, I wanted to walk straight to the stage. I had never stopped thinking about Kevin Brennan's offer to vouch for me. It was the kind of opportunity every comedian waits for. Not every comedian says, "Thank you, but give me a year."

I didn't question my comedic ability. I questioned my ability, period. A stranger believed in me more than I believed in myself. Before stand-up, I had never had a measurable skill. Even my mom could only come up with that I was "good with people," a compliment reserved for friendly dogs. She was my greatest defender and would annually present the argument to my teachers that I shouldn't be forced to repeat whatever grade I was about to fail. She would insist I was smart—I just had a yet-to-be-determined problem. My teachers felt they had pinpointed the issue. They were convinced I took so long to read and write because I was lazy, which is as logical as suspecting an alcoholic drinks so much because they're thirsty. Looking at the zero-out-of-ten spelling test results and thinking, "The boy is idle," is as ignorant as observing a flaming car wreck and concluding, "The driver must have been parched."

The school system treats neurodiverse students so badly, we need a lifetime of deprogramming. Dyslexics have to forge our own path. We're different. More important than dyslexics succeeding in school is their self-esteem remaining intact throughout the process. Kids need to know that, with a slight change of parameters, dyslexia has been proven to be a positive. If I could pick a standard brain or a unique one, I would pick mine. Every time.

Given the option to move at my own pace, I found success. When I had extra time to take my finals with Mr. Armstrong in the Learning Resource Center, I'd aced those exams. With stand-up, I didn't need an extra year to improve. I needed time for my belief in myself to catch up to my ability. And I wouldn't walk down into the hallowed basement of the Comedy Cellar until my self-belief aligned with my skill. Until I was ready.

———

The DJ and the actress moved to Los Angeles, as DJs and actors tend to do. While they packed up their turntables and ring lights, Dutch sensed something was up, sat on my feet, and cried. Roommates forty-two and forty-three were a biblical scholar and an eighty-two-year-old woman named Erma.

Erma had a rent-controlled unit in the Westbeth Artists Community next to the West Side Highway. The building had once housed Bell Laboratories, where scientists had invented the quartz electronic clock, transatlantic telephone service, and had helped develop the atomic bomb. It's also the location where I wrote some bangers.

Most of the current occupants were as old as those inventions. In 1970, Westbeth had been established with the plan that a group of artists would move out every five years, and a new group would replace them. One of the artists happened to have gone to law school and found a loophole in the contract. Erma and the first group of artists never left. Now the building functioned as a de facto old age home and an untapped sitcom premise.

Erma and I lived on the main floor, our rooms separated by a large living room. The biblical scholar lived upstairs in a room I called the pulpit. Erma had mobility issues, which made her a bit of a homebody. She was partial to the Home and Garden network but was always eager to hit Mute and chat. "You'll never guess who slept on this couch," she said one afternoon.

"Ethel Merman," I shot back.

"What do you know about her?" She giggled. "Miles Davis's son."

"What?"

"Gil Evans, Miles's piano player, lived across the hall. When I came home one night, Miles's son was sleeping in the hall in front of Gil's door. I said, 'Come on, you can sleep here.' We shared a can of soup and when I woke up, he was gone. So was the spare change I kept in here." She chuckled and pointed at the wooden bowl on the coffee table. "Ethel Merman, you're daft."

A lifelong New Yorker, Erma always had a story. One night she hit Mute on *Property Brothers* and told me, "You know the walkway on the other side of the West Side Highway? That's where the *New York Times* used to park their delivery trucks. At night prostitutes would bring their johns. They'd work out of the back."

"Is that where paper boys became paper men?" I asked.

She smiled and motioned the channel changer in my direction. "I wish I could mute you, mister."

The biblical scholar was a hulk of a man in his fifties. When he wasn't toiling on a writing project that Erma referred to as an unabridged version of the Old Testament, he was being handy around the apartment. He had built my loft bed. He once cornered me in the kitchen and took me through the entire building procedure while I considered climbing down the garbage disposal in search of a more pleasant experience. Our friendship peaked one morning when he pointed at my Grateful Dead T-shirt and asked if I was a fan.

"They're my lifeblood," I said.

"Well, I attended a wonderful performance."

I hadn't seen that coming.

"My younger brother Luke is a Deadhead and we attended."

"What year?"

"This is remarkable," he commented. "I've never seen you so spirited."

Well, I thought, you're not giving a dissertation on deck nails.

"It was eighty-nine," he said.

"Prime time."

"Well, I don't know about that. But I will say the religious parallels were uncanny. The Deadheads are disciples."

"The most spiritual moments of my life have been at shows," I said.

"I felt very uplifted by the lyrics. Not unlike after a sermon. I was suspicious of the biblical parallels. It was all confirmed by their encore."

I love Dead trivia, but not as much as he liked the sound of his own voice. He answered before I could guess. "'Knocking on Heaven's Door.' It was phenomenal."

Right when I was thinking maybe I'd been wrong about him, he said, "Now I need to talk to you about the manner in which you're walking up the stairs. You're wearing out the paint. I need you to lift your feet more. You're shuffling like a toddler. May I show you the ideal method to ascend?"

"I'm good."

"Well, I would simply mention it in a note, but with your affliction

I know reading is not part of your skill set. I suppose you could hold up a mirror so you could see the letters correctly."

Concepts like these—that dyslexics see things backward, and that we can't entirely read—are based on uninformed stereotypes. Some jerk wrote "dyslexics untie" on a bathroom stall and then everyone was like, "Got it, thanks for encapsulating that complex learning disability."

———

Later that night, I dodged crowds in Times Square. On the sidewalk beneath a digital billboard advertising McFlurrys, guys in Timberlands and puffer jackets barked at tourists.

"Dave Chappelle tonight at the World Comedy Cafe," yelled a guy with a neck tattoo of a name I couldn't read. "We got Chris Rock filming his new special tonight."

"That's right, Chris Rock," called another barker.

Barking wasn't a thing in Vancouver. In New York, it was a rite of passage. Some of the people trying to drum up an audience were open mic-ers forced to hand out flyers for stage time. Customers brought the flyer to the club with the barker's signature. Six paying customers earned five minutes. The other barkers were the club's "street team." I overheard one guy tell his partner he'd spent last night in Rikers.

In Vancouver, I had studied the websites of all the comedy clubs in Manhattan but had never heard of the World Comedy Cafe. For good reason. It was above the Broadway Comedy Club, a "B" room in New York. Inside, the club was filled with tourists who'd forgotten to get Broadway tickets. Or maybe dyslexics who'd bought tickets to a show the week after their trip. A lot of fanny packs and confused faces. To maximize profits, the owner had placed tables on the stage. Servers awkwardly stepped around the performers, taking drink orders mid-set. I had been through a lot to be on this stage. These people were just gullible in Times Square.

Because I had TV credits, I didn't have to bark and closed the show. When the host brought me up as "the last comic of the night," the crowd suddenly came to terms with the fact that Chris Rock was not filming a comedy special in a club with no cameras. Rough shows were nothing new, but I had never performed as part of a ruse.

During my set, I noticed a distressed woman in the front row. "Is everything okay?" I asked.

"Everything is not okay," she said. "This is our last night of vacation. Instead of going to a Broadway show, we came here because they promised Chris Rock and Dave Chappelle. When we got here, we were charged sixteen dollars for drinks made with fake alcohol."

She was making strong points. My sympathy overrode the urge to be funny. "I'm really sorry," I said.

"We just want to go home."

I reached into my pocket, pulled out forty dollars, and put it on her table. "Let me pay for your fake drinks," I said.

The crowd was silent.

"Don't worry, it's counterfeit."

For months, I did five shows a night on weekends and two shows a night on weekdays at the World. It paid nothing; I didn't even get a free drink. Between shows, I walked around Hell's Kitchen. When it got late and sketchy, I sat in a bodega that for some reason had a few tables and chairs, watching people stumble in on their way to nightclubs. Women often asked if they could join me while they applied Band-Aids to the injuries caused by disagreeable shoes. One night at the World's early show, I shut down a female heckler, and her husband, who looked like a mobster, threatened to kill me. After a death threat, it's hard to make the audience sympathize with the difficulty of sexting when you have a learning disability. I walked to my bodega and called my mom, needing to hear a supportive voice. But my dad answered the phone.

"Hello?"

"Hi." My tone was telling.

"Oh," my dad said. "That doesn't sound good."

"It's not. I'm so sick of this shit. Pardon my language. The crowds suck."

"So you just had a bad set."

"It's more than that. It feels pointless. There's like six tables on the stage. At the early show tonight, during my closer, a woman told me her bill was wrong. Like I'm the waiter."

"Delph, you got to get out of that hellhole. You need to take your friend up on his offer about the Cellar."

I regretted telling him about Kevin Brennan's offer.

"You moved all the way to New York for that exact opportunity," he went on. "And you won't pull the trigger. It's been a year and a half."

"Ten and a half months."

"What are you waiting for?"

"I'm getting the rhythm of the crowds here," I said.

"Oh, that's bullshit," my dad said.

"I'm scared I'm going to mess it up," I admitted.

"That's bullshit too. This is all because of what those pecker-heads did to you in school. You have to leave that behind. It's done. The booker at the Cellar isn't going to give you a spelling test. You're getting tested on what you're great at. We were watching some-one on Netflix the other night . . . damn, I forgot his name . . . anyways, he couldn't carry your pen. My point is, call your friend."

"I gotta go. I have one more miserable spot," I said.

"Okay, Delph, but think about what I said. Prove those asshole teachers wrong."

At the World, I found the manager, whose job was to tell barkers they couldn't perform because they sold five tickets instead of six. "Hey, we're running forty-five minutes late," he said. "That's only the second guy."

Onstage, a comic did one-handed push-ups while the crowd counted in unison. I sat at the back of the room and was flooded with a memory from the beginning of first grade. Mrs. Skeen collected the spelling tests and saw that I got zero and I'd marked Danny Birch's test incorrectly. She turned red, slammed her hand down on her desk, and shouted, "Philip, you can't do anything right." Then she stomped across the classroom, grabbed my desk with my little body still in it, and dragged it across the room. Only the back legs of the desk and the tippy toes of my sneakers touched the linoleum floor. She slammed it down facing the back wall.

"If you turn around you'll wish we never met," she screamed, so close to my face that I could smell the cigarette-and-coffee combination that polluted her breath.

She then composed herself and announced to everyone: "In all my years of teaching there's always only been two reading groups. The A word group and the B word group. But now because Philip can't keep up we're going to have a third reading group just for him called the C word group."

Tonight, I was still stuck at the back of the room. But now I realized my teacher had named my group after herself. And I realized that was a bit and scribbled it down on the back of my set list. Then I pulled out my phone and texted Kevin Brennan: "I'm ready."

Text bubbles appeared on my phone screen.

"Are you wet?"

14

Home

I reach the Olive Tree, the restaurant above the Comedy Cellar, fifteen minutes before my spot. I make my way up the five steps, past
the customers eating and drinking, and sit down at the comics' table,
in the back of the room, where the comedians wait to be summoned
downstairs for their sets. I sit down, pull out a legal pad, fold a page
in half, and work on my set list. I write in gigantic misshapen letters
that have been compared to hieroglyphics. Because I can't spell—or
can't remember how most words are spelled—I write them phonet-
ically. Every time I write a word, I do it differently. Which, in a way,
is more impressive. I can spell most words fifteen different ways.
Halfway through my set list, which could be mistaken for a cryptic
ransom note, Sam Morril slides up next to me and jokingly grabs
one of my legal pages and quips, "in case anyone ever questioned
that you had a learning disability."

I laugh too. I now wear my dyslexia as a badge of honor. I talk
about it every night to hundreds of people, sometimes thousands.
Yes, it owns me, but now I own it too. As a comic, I am a proud

member of a community of misfits that laughs at my differences and my emotional battle scars. We celebrate them. I know I wouldn't be where I am without them. The New York comics have come to expect my giant notes and the sight of rolled-up butcher paper sticking out of my backpack. One recently looked into the bottom of my book bag, saw the set list and random notes, and inquired if I had a hamster.

I've been in New York for years. My first week working at the Cellar, I got thirteen spots. At the greatest club on the planet. A far cry from the music open mics and the underground swinger clubs of Vancouver. Instead of risking my life driving through the Canadian Rockies to get to a dreadful one-nighter, I now stroll ten minutes through the Village to get to the club I used to watch on TV while having dinner with my mom.

I've had the privilege of becoming friends with some of the best and most inspiring comics working. After years of watching Colin Quinn hanging out at the Cellar in *Comedian*, I now often find myself living that scene. It's not only dinner we share; we have the same manager, Brian Stern. One night soon after I got passed at the Cellar, I noticed Amy Schumer eyeing me suspiciously. "I can't understand why you're a comic," she said.

"What do you mean?" I asked.

"You're too normal; you have a jawline," she said. "There's no part of you that's broken."

When she found out I was dyslexic, it clicked. There it was. My wound. And also my bow.

One night while hanging out on the steps in front of the club in between sets, I met the new general manager, whose name is Liz. She had worked at the Cellar for years, left, and then had come back. Liz soon became instrumental in helping my life run smoothly. Her younger sister is dyslexic. She knows exactly what it entails and now does everything from updating my website to producing my comedy special. She's beyond clutch. I love her the way I love other people who always seem to save the day, like Ronnie and Pugs.

And Liz sprang into action when a relationship ended abruptly. How abruptly? Well, I woke up in the apartment I had shared with my girlfriend of three years, who did a bang-up job of spell-checking my correspondence (for a fee, but still!), and when I arrived at the Cellar that night I had to get my stuff out of my ex-girlfriend's place. By the time I was being brought onstage, Liz had arranged for two comedians to come by the apartment the next day to pick up my stuff. During my set, I saw Liz whispering with Amy Schumer. When I walked offstage, Amy pulled me aside and said, "I want you to come stay with me." The next morning Liz provided moral support as I searched Marshalls for the biggest suitcase they had. "Throw on a pair of sunglasses," she advised. "We both know there's going to be enough tears to get you admitted into a women's shelter."

My heart heals rapidly in Amy's Upper West Side penthouse, where I've been living for six months. The Comedy Cellar is no longer a dream; it is becoming my extended family. I am still living in Amy's luxe accommodations when I am approached by a literary agent. He asks if I am interested in writing a book about dyslexia. My initial reaction is that sounds like the worst *Shark Tank* pitch ever.

When I ask Amy what she thinks of the idea, she responds, "Why the fuck not?"

One day, I arrive at Le Grainne Cafe in Chelsea. Shalom is already there. I haven't seen my old friend in fifteen years, maybe longer. For no precise reason—I still love her and think about her frequently. We're both from Oshawa. Both left at a young age. I've never forgotten how instrumental she was in my escape. If our hometown was a prison, she smuggled in a file. Shalom gives me a familiar hug.

"Oh my God I missed you," she says.

"It's so good to see you."

Our connection is tangible. Shalom tells me she has had years of health problems but is finally on the mend. I feel guilty that I wasn't there for her while she was sick. On the French server's fifth attempt, we're ready to give her our order. We both get salads. It's so good to see her, food feels insignificant.

"How's your mom?" I ask. "How's Sandy?"

Shalom reaches across the table and grabs my hand. "My mom died," she says.

"Wha . . ."

Before I get to the *t*, I burst into tears. I cry in a way I haven't cried since my nervous breakdown. The news hits me like a sucker punch to the solar plexus. We both jump to our feet and embrace, even tighter this time.

"It's okay, baby," Shalom says. "It's okay."

I feel like I should be supporting her, but I can't pull it together.

Sandy was a remarkable person. When I was a teenager, she told me I had charisma. She was sincere and made me feel recognized and special when I needed it most. The last time I saw her, my parents still lived in Oshawa. She had broken her hip and I dropped off a puzzle of tropical fish.

Two nights later Shalom comes to the Comedy Cellar. As we walk down the stairs from the Olive Tree to the showroom, she observes, "It wouldn't be an Oshawa hang if it wasn't in a basement."

I ask the manager to get her a seat on the floaters, the Cellar's version of a VIP section. I'm often nervous when someone comes to watch me. Not Shalom. I feel mighty. I realize that technically she was at my very first shows in the Love brothers' basement. As I work the crowd, I can hear Shalom's laugh, which gives me even more confidence. When I come off the stage, she embraces me.

"I almost peed myself," Shalom proclaims. "I'm so proud of you. You're a lovable asshole."

I've gone from entertaining my friends in a basement on Carnaby Crescent in Oshawa, Ontario, to entertaining them in a basement that is world renowned.

Pugs is still around. Still my best friend. We talk every week, and he comes to catch my show whenever he can. He's still low-key. In 2015, the remaining members of the Grateful Dead celebrated their fiftieth anniversary by playing three sold-out concerts at Chicago's Soldier Field. We attended together. Upon arriving, everyone was given a rose. My rose is preserved on my bookshelf. Pugs gave his to the woman who sold him the first of many giant beers.

The third night concluded with an incredible version of "Attics of My Life." As the musicians sang a capella, photos of the band appeared on the screen, including Papa Bear himself, Jerry Garcia. Pugs's were the only dry eyes in the house. I credit dyslexia for my love of the Grateful Dead, who've touched me in a way that only the greatest art can. My learning disability gave me the context that leads to empathy. As a teenager, I believed Jerry when he sang,

Kid can't read at seventeen
The words he knows are all obscene
but it's all right
I will get by
I will get by
I will get by
I will survive

Jerry was right. I survived.

The Dead community describes this weekend as the celebration of a lifetime. Pugs's take? "Yeah, it was pretty good." His even-keeled nature is why it means so much to me when I'm in his room and notice he has a framed set list from a show I did ten years ago. The only decoration in his entire two-bedroom condo.

I still consider Ronnie a best friend, even with what feels like more years than miles of ocean since the last time I've seen him. But we are still in contact. When I told him that Marty, now fifteen, is into mod culture, the youth movement born in England in the late '50s, Ronnie promptly dropped a vintage mod parka in the mail. When I thanked him, he blew it off: "Phylicia, we can't have

the young lad walking around in a naff Canadian parka, can we?"
I heard him pour a glass of wine. "Ah," Ronnie said. "That's lovely."

Marty and I have a freakish connection that my last girlfriend
envied. She took issue with our nightly two-hour chats from when
he was nine till he turned thirteen. My prayers worked. Marty's
not dyslexic. He reads well and frequently. We share the same favorite
author. But I was too specific in my plea to the universe: Marty has
dyscalculia. He struggles with math the way I struggle with words.
He shares my hatred for school and so many of my other traits that
Patty and my mom mix up our names in conversation frequently
enough that people have stopped correcting them. They just look for
other clues in the sentence, knowing Marty's not likely to be playing
Denver this weekend and it's doubtful that Phil has to be home by
10:30 sharp.

Today I continue to deal with dyslexia. But it's no longer a battle. I've made peace. I work around it. Every time I need to mail
something, I go to this specialty post office, a place that charges
double the regular price, but one of the sisters who runs it has a
dyslexic boyfriend. I can show her a screenshot of the address I
need something to go to, and she'll write it all out. The prices are
astronomical, but my mail arrives where I intend it to. Which is
priceless. Over time I've learned these strategies. The most merciful
thing time has done is erode the shame that has been linked to my
disability since my first visit to Mrs. Simmons's Learning Resource
Center in the first grade.

I'm reminded of those days when I speak at an event for Eye to
Eye, an organization whose mission is to improve the educational

experiences and outcomes of neurodiverse young people. In a large solarium-like room at the University of Denver, I watch the students file in. They are taking part in a week of leadership building. Although the week is filled with fun events, most arrive with their shoulders slumped, gazing at the ground. A look I know well.

I perform fifteen minutes of stand-up comedy. Performing dyslexic material to dyslexic students makes me feel like Bob Hope entertaining the troops, because these kids are still in the trenches. After my set, one of the team leaders asks standard questions about how I got started in comedy and how I come up with material. I rush through my answers. I have something I need to say. The thing I wish someone had told me.

I tell the students that the school system is not designed for us. The way a monster truck track is not made for NASCAR. It's not our fault. Schools need to change. So do society's views on people with dyslexia. I know firsthand that students' learning problems are often overlooked or dealt with incorrectly. I offer them encouragement. I share with them that until my final year of high school, the only reassurance I ever got from teachers when they found out I was dyslexic was, "Hey, Tom Cruise is dyslexic," to which I responded, "Oh cool, well then I'll just star in *Top Gun*."

When the moderator opens it up to questions, I anticipate being asked if I've ever met Kevin Hart. One by one, students raise their hands and ask a variation of the same query. *How are you not ashamed? Why aren't you embarrassed to tell people you're dyslexic?*

I do my best to vary the wording of my answers. I say I've completely stopped feeling shame the way a snake sheds its skin. It's simply no longer there. Unlike a snake, though, I no longer slither and hide. I welcome opportunities to address my disability. In fact, I sometimes shoehorn it into conversations. Besides the Grateful Dead and vintage watches, dyslexia is my favorite topic. I suspect the shift started when I was released from school. The upside of dyslexia—my creativity, my humor, my lightheartedness, my drive—was allowed to reveal itself. I no longer felt defeated. School suppressed my strengths. When I left, every day felt like a Saturday.

After the talk, I stand off to the side and speak with David Flink, the founder and CEO of Eye to Eye. The teenagers, who are supposed to be taking part in a neurodiverse invasion of a local go-kart track, line up in front of me. One by one, they try to get me to shed some light on this no shame thing.

One girl fights back tears while she confesses her study process. She has to sit on the floor and work on giant pieces of poster board. Although I'm heartbroken by her story, I am inspired by her ingenuity. She talks about her process in a hushed, confessional tone, the way a drug addict might describe the daily hassle and hustle of scoring their fix. Like drug addicts, dyslexics face a lifetime of people who will never walk a mile in their shoes but are quick to give flippant directions. To laymen, spell-check and books on tape seem to be cure-alls. These solutions are about as helpful as telling a drug addict to "Just say no."

I tell the girl I do the same thing. When it comes to my stand-up, I don't write jokes. I draw them on a giant whiteboard. When a joke is ready to be tested onstage, it is named and relocated to a floor-to-ceiling piece of butcher paper that hangs beside the whiteboard. With the Grateful Dead playing in the background, I pace around the whiteboard, talking to myself as I sketch out my jokes. Most comics carry a tiny notebook, usually Moleskine brand, where they jot down all their ideas and jokes. I can't fathom fitting letters and words between those dainty lines. To me it's like building a ship in a bottle. I have to use giant canvases. And because I spell words differently every time, I have to decipher my own notes, like that main character in *Memento*, waking up every morning searching for the person he was the day before. I tell the girl that earlier in my life, the shame of being different would have stopped me. It doesn't anymore.

More kids come up to me. Each has their own story, but the stories are all eerily similar to mine. The big difference is these kids can't seem to quite understand that I walk around with my head held high. They don't just envy my shamelessness; they have trouble comprehending it.

I challenge the kids to try to go a full week without hesitating to ask people for help the way I do at my overpriced post office. I suggest a version of the exposure therapy that I learned to cope with my OCD. Talking to them reinforces how important it is to recognize how much members of the neurodiverse community struggle in school, and how courageous they are to face adversity day in and day out. It's far more impressive than someone who can answer a series of multiple-choice questions correctly because they memorized some text.

I try to convince these kids that dyslexia is not a curse. It can be a huge pain in the ass, but having it does not spell certain condemnation (nor can I, without the help of Google). Quite the opposite, in fact. Bob Weir of the Grateful Dead is dyslexic. And the guy *owns* it. He'll cover a Bob Dylan song and get every lyric right, but then he'll do another song he's done forever and get totally lost and just shrug, and the audience loves it. That was a powerful lesson for me. If you watch him play guitar, his fingering, his whole approach, is so unconventional, his time signatures so unique, unlike anyone else's. He didn't succeed despite his dyslexia, but because of it. It's imperative that kids who struggle are shown a light at the end of the tunnel. Otherwise, their current misery will seem everlasting.

I'm someone who can tell these kids, "Hey, look at me—I love my life and have the 'mighty D' to thank." Because as much as we've learned about dyslexia and raised its profile, we have a long, long way to go. I know if I went back to a shitty town in Canada, I'd find a miserable third grader with a teacher who's not only failing to teach but also causing senseless damage to this kid's self-worth. And although it's that teacher's shortcomings that should be brought into question, it's the innocent dyslexic student who will be chastised and belittled.

After the event, David Flink tells me, "There's something to that seven-day shameless challenge."

"Really? It's so cathartic talking to dyslexics. It was a personal struggle for so long, like I was the only one who experienced this stuff."

"We all go through it, I'm afraid," David says.

"I hate that they are burdened with shame. It breaks my heart.

I almost cried talking to that girl. I always tell parents of dyslexic kids to maintain their self-esteem."

"I do the same."

"What do you say?"

"I say validate their humanity. Give them an authentic compliment about something they're good at. If it's building things with Legos, then recognize it."

"I've told parents that they have to be so careful about their kid doing activities outside of school. They need to remember that school for us is a letter sweatshop," I say. "They have to be gentle. They can't force them to practice the harp for three hours."

David chuckles. "Letter sweatshop. I like that. What did your parents do?" he asks.

"They recognized I was funny at the dinner table. They celebrated it. And my dad called my teachers peckerheads. He told me I was smarter than them."

David smiles.

"Whatever they did, it worked."

He's right. When I look at my life it's impossible to still think of dyslexia as a curse. I look at the things I cherish most about my life and I can connect them all to my disability, especially my relationship with my mom. We have a bond that only two people who have been through something as a team and triumphed can share. She's still my top supporter at eighty years old. She loves my comedy, and she knows how many spots I got at the Cellar this week. She followed how many views came in on a viral Instagram clip, even though she's not super clear on what Instagram is all about. When I told her I was starting a book proposal, she said, "I'm worried that it will cause stress for you, dear. But I'm proud that you always set such high goals for yourself. I know when you set your mind to something you achieve it." I'm not throwing my books off the kitchen table anymore, but I still bitch and complain about being dyslexic to her. And she has the same sympathetic "oh, dear" response she's always had.

Now when I'm the center of attention, I don't stutter or stumble. I speak directly, with pride. Now people laugh with me. Dyslexia doesn't alienate me anymore: it connects. Instead of praying each night that I'll wake up with a different brain, I feel gratitude for the one I have. I realize that God listened to me all those years ago and I did indeed wake up smart.

Because after all, it's my dyslexic material that people want to discuss at meet and greets after the shows. It turns out I'm not remotely the only one. Nondyslexic fans appreciate my honesty and relate it to their own struggles, even if they're far removed from reading difficulties. Audiences are used to hearing filthy sex material, but I'll go on about my experiences in education, and people are engaged, even the drunks. I'll ask if anyone in the crowd is dyslexic. I can tell by looking at those who raise their hands if they've had a hard life. Most have. I'll look at them and think about the kids I was in special ed with, and wonder where they are now.

Many years have passed since the agonizing days of school, but time doesn't distance me from the memories. The feelings of inadequacy, injustice, and frustration are still right there. The intro of the Sunday night news program *60 Minutes*, with its stopwatch imagery and hypnotic ticking sound, still brings me back to the disheartening realization that my weekend is over and school, the worst and longest part of the loop that was my life, is about to start. It still gives me anxiety. Monday mornings back then, my first thought was, oh no. Then I'd try to comfort myself by thinking that after today, I only had four days left. Every Wednesday I'd tell myself, "Tomorrow I'll be able to say tomorrow is Friday." Saturday was really the only reprieve. Sunday felt like the eve of doom. So now when I see kids with book bags heading to school, I hope they've been spared. Statistically, though, I know that some must have learning disabilities. I just pray they have a Barbara Joan Hanley. Someone who is perpetually in their corner and at the kitchen table.

When I finished school, the loop unfolded and became linear. Being forced to do something I hated every day led to finding my passion. But I also know that my story is uncommon. In the United States, 10 percent of the general population is dyslexic. And a groundbreaking study done in Texas in 2000 showed that 48 percent of prison inmates studied there showed signs of dyslexia. Twenty-one years later, another study in Louisiana prisons again found that 47 percent of inmates studied had dyslexia; 97 percent had been in special ed. Ninety-fucking-seven percent. I am heartbroken but not surprised by these statistics. When you're asked to do something like read, something that most people do effortlessly and that you simply can't do, it affects how you feel about yourself and it also affects how you feel about the world. It feels so unfair to be mocked, belittled, isolated, and publicly shamed for not having a skill like reading, especially because it's not for lack of trying. We're just not hardwired for the task, the way not every kid can throw a curveball or make the perfect flan. That frustration builds, and it is human nature to lash out—to shoplift or vandalize something with misspelled graffiti. How would adults behave if they were belittled at work daily by their boss for something completely out of their hands? "Your sales are abysmal." "I work in accounting."

———

One Sunday night after my set at the Comedy Cellar, I walk up the stairs and find my friend Zach Zimmerman sitting at the comics table by himself.

"Zachary," I say, happy to see him.

"How are they down there?"

"They're hot, man. You're going to have a blast."

"It's so weird. I was just thinking about you," Zach says. "There's a woman sitting over there, and it just popped into my head that you would find her attractive."

I assume she's Indian. I dated one Indian woman and have a few jokes about our relationship and the ensuing breakup. She ended things in a text, which is mean to do to anyone, but particularly to a dyslexic. I suspect her mom had played a part in the breakup. She had deemed me subhuman because I didn't attend college. She had proclaimed that I had an unstable job, only to find her company downsizing and herself out of work. My point is, I'm completely over it.

I look across the restaurant. A woman with blond hair sitting with a large group stares back at me. When our eyes meet, I feel overwhelmed and look back at Zach.

"Blond hair?" I ask.

"That's her," he says, knowing he nailed it.

The show's host, Jon Laster, beckons Zach downstairs for his set. I get up to head around the block to one of the Cellar's other venues, the Village Underground, for my last spot of the night. The blond woman stands as I approach. When she smiles, I realize she's even more stunning than I thought.

"Hey, I was at the show on Friday," she says. "I loved your set."

"Oh, thank you. I'm Phil."

"I know," she says, smiling. "Emma. You're from Canada, right? I love Canada."

"You've been to Canada?"

"Vancouver for work a couple times."

"That's where my parents live. Where are you from?"

"North Carolina."

"I love Charleston," I exclaim.

She smiles. "That's South Carolina."

"Well, I guess it depends where you're coming from."

She laughs and touches my arm. Holy fuck, I think to myself.

"People in the South remind me of Canadians," I say.

"Because we're polite, but we're also a lot of other things," she confesses.

"You seem to have kept all the best parts of the South."

She smiles even wider. I have the urge to high-five myself.

"I have another spot around the block, but we should get a drink sometime."

Her expression changes. "Um, I . . ." she stutters.

"I just meant as friends," I say, trying to recover.

"Yes, okay," she says as I realize I'm going to be late for my spot.

"It was nice meeting you," I say. "Add me on Instagram."

"Nice meeting you too. I will for sure," she says and sits back down with her friends.

As I turn down West Third Street I see Liz standing out in front of the Village Underground. "You're cutting it fucking close," she says as I run past her and head downstairs.

"Liz, I love you," I yell over my shoulder.

Before calling Marty to say good night, I scold myself for asking Emma out and making her uncomfortable. I completely blew it. I still haven't forgiven myself while I'm drinking my second and final Sleepytime tea. Then I notice I've gotten a direct message on Instagram.

"I meant what I said. You were my favorite of the night," Emma writes. "I'm not on here much but here is my number."

I click on her profile and notice millions of followers. She is an actor, and I have seen and enjoyed some of her work. Ronnie would call me "a donut." Pugs, "a dizzy son of a bitch." I scroll further and see someone who appears to be her partner. Probably a reader who went to college. Someone her southern parents are over the moon about.

The next day I text Emma: "It was nice meeting you and thank you for your kind words."

There's a bit of back and forth, but then things peter out. By the end of the afternoon, I'm convinced I will never see her again and that dyslexia also affects my ability to read social situations.

I've recently realized that the wound and bow theory applies to more than just dyslexia. It's every struggle. The bigger the battle, the more you invest, the greater the payoff. The rough stand-up gigs I did early in my career toughened me up. They made me over-qualified to handle minor incidents that occur at regular comedy shows. A heckle is nothing when you have faced potential violence. For years I played places that were so bad, the consensus among the customers was "he must suck if he's performing here." Shows where the only way I could get their attention was if I addressed an audience member directly. If I didn't, they wouldn't look at me. Sometimes they wouldn't even face the stage.

I thought I was just surviving. I was actually developing part of my act that would help me turn a corner. I've started posting crowd-work clips on Instagram and YouTube. Some have gone viral, leading to people finally buying tickets to my shows on tour. The beauty is that I am capturing things that would otherwise be forgotten forever, like Deadheads taping thousands of live shows. Liz from the Cellar has been on me to post clips for years. Because crowd work is one of the rare, rare things that always came easy, I used to devalue it. If I could do it, it must not be remarkable. I never thought it would be the thing that would gain me a following and help me start selling out weekends. But now I've come to recognize and celebrate my innate gifts.

One day I wake up to a text from Emma. It has been a couple months, and I haven't been able to shake that first conversation or the feeling I got when we first locked eyes. She says that she had a dream about me and although the details are vague, she's ready for that friendly drink.

We arrange to meet at my favorite date spot that happens to be on my street. It's one of those pretentious cocktail bars that are hard to get into. But I know the doorman. His dad is an OG Deadhead and he likes that I still represent the boys.

Emma and I arrive at the same time. I can't believe how good it feels to talk to her. The only thing I can compare it to is running down a hill. My mouth can't keep up with the information I feel compelled to share with her. I even mention the book proposal, something that I don't really tell people, especially ones I've just met. After my second Negroni, my current limit, I put my hand on top of hers. She smiles and squeezes it.

"Friendly drink," she reminds me.

"I was about to remind you of the same thing."

Emma laughs. "I really like you. Like I'm surprised how much I like you, but I just ended a relationship, and if I started a new one without dealing with the residuals of the last, it wouldn't be fair," she explains.

I don't care for her honesty.

"Well, if we're being honest." I pause. She's still holding my hand. "I don't want to drink anymore, but I still want to hang out. Do you want to go to my place?"

"Okay," she says with a shrug.

When we arrive at my apartment building, Emma cackles. "You have to be joking," she says as I turn the key.

"What?" I ask defensively.

"Oh boy," she says. "You live two doors down."

As we walk up the five floors to my apartment, she proceeds to roast me for meeting her in a bar "that's in the basement of your building."

"What if I told you I was concerned about my carbon footprint?" I ask.

"I would say you're full of shit," she answers.

I open the door and the ball busting continues. "You tidied," she says sarcastically.

I thought I did. My dyslexic disorganization is compounded by my minuscule apartment. With romance off the table, we continue to chat and laugh, and, at one point, Emma dances the Charleston. I let her wear one of my watches, a 1970 Rolex 1675 GMT Master with perfect custard-colored lume. Purchasing it finally took the sting out of giving Armani his watch back all those years ago.

"Oh my God it's three a.m.," she says when she puts it on. "I got to go."

I walk her the two steps to my door. "Please don't try to make out with me," I say.

"We'll hug."

Her hug makes all other hugs seem obsolete.

"I hated that," I tell her.

"Me too," she says, squeezing my hand again before disappearing down the stairs.

I lie in my bed with a grin as I replay the night until my phone buzzes. "I got home safe. You're officially my hottest friend."

"Same," I reply.

Our friendship goes on for over a year before it becomes something much much more.

During that time I work hard. I focus the way I focused in my last year of high school. Instead of trying to prove something to a pessimistic guidance counselor who would ultimately apologize for not believing in me, I'm working to prove something to myself. I feel like if I can accomplish this one thing, I will once and for all leave behind all the damage, self-doubt, and resentment. This one thing will make my nervous breakdown, my failed relationships, my insufferable roommates, the impossible crowds, the lonely travel, and the nights I didn't get to kiss Marty good night worthwhile. It will say to the few people who believed in me that they were right and to the people who didn't: fuck you.

I've worked on this fifty-page book proposal for four years. Its working title is *War and Piece*. The day after I give it to my manager, I am on the road in Springfield, Missouri, and receive a call from Colin Quinn. "I hear you nailed the proposal," he says in his ironic New York accent. "Brian says it's really great."

Colin's call fills me with an unfamiliar feeling of confidence. Not the kind I might get from a good set where I can credit a hot crowd or my placement in the show. This feels different. I find myself struck by the thought, Wait, what if publishers feel the same way? To even have that thought is audacious for someone whose reading and writing skills are such that I've never chosen a glass of wine for myself at a restaurant. My whole life, my order has been "I'll get the same."

Later that week, I do what I always do when there's an important event in my life, good or bad: I call my mom.

"Hello," she says.

"Hi Ma."

"Oh, hi dear."

"I sold the book."

"You did! Martin, Martin. Delphi sold the book."

I celebrate at my favorite Italian restaurant with Estee and my friend, comedian Matteo Lane. Estee toasts me and my accomplishment in her slight Israeli accent. "Here's to coming a long way," she says.

"And selling your book," Matteo adds.

I clink my glass of "I'll get the same" and think back to the time I was called on by my third-grade teacher, Mrs. Douglas, to read out loud in front of the class. I couldn't get the first word. Like an old car that wouldn't start, it just wasn't happening. Instead of doing what she normally did, humiliate me for a bit before moving on, Mrs. Douglas decided to turn the screws and ask, "If you can't read or write, how are you going to pay your bills?" How I wish I could transport myself back to that moment. I know how miraculous it would be, how good it would feel, if I could be eight years old again and answer with conviction, "Well, Mrs. Douglas, the truth is, I'll make money by talking shit about you."

Yep. I wouldn't change a thing.

Acknowledgments

Thank you to my family, Martin, Joan, Patricia, Marty, and Trevor, for their support and for instilling me with enough confidence to attempt this project. When I first left home to go to Milan to model, my dad sensed I was nervous and said, "You go, and if it doesn't work out, you come home, where you're always a hero."

Thank you to my manager, Brian Stern, for believing in me all these years. It was Brian and my literary agent, Ethan Bassoff, who came up with the whimsical idea that their dyslexic client should write a memoir. I'm grateful to them both. Thank you to Kailan for teaching me that "loud marks" are called exclamation points. And to Alex Brizel for your daily diligence, and taking the baton from one of the greats, Andrew Bloom. Thank you to Megan Muralles for your daily check-ins via voice memo.

Huge thanks to James Melia for acquiring *Spellbound*. And to Serena Jones for helping me get it over the finish line and supporting my vision for every aspect of the book. Also, many thanks to the whole Henry Holt team: Zoë Affron, Caitlin Mulrooney-Lyski,

Sam Wiener, and Guy Oldfield. Christopher Sergio, Ian Koviak, and Alan Dino Hebel designed such an incredible cover and entertained me by saying things like, "I want it to look like Saul Bass doodled it while listening to the Grateful Dead." Thank you to my dyslexic friend and phenomenal photographer Matt Salacuse for taking my jacket photo.

My stand-up agent, Tommy Pucciani, helps me get onstage and do what I love and always looks for an opportunity for me to check out a Dead show in between gigs. Cyn saved the day when getting an NYC hotel was out of reach. Noam Dworman and Estee Adoram welcomed me into the Comedy Cellar family. Thank you to Liz Furiati for the immaculate job she does as the chief operating officer of my life. The mighty Colin Quinn showed me that comics can do more than stand-up. During the ups and downs of life, I often remind myself: at least I'm friends with Colin Quinn. John Wing was the first pro to believe in and encourage me at a time when it meant so much. Thank you to Bart Coleman for the breaks and for having impeccable taste in music and to Molly Schminke for headlining an unknown Canadian and accompanying me to see the boys at Shoreline. I'm grateful to Amy Schumer for showing me generosity over the years. It was in "our" kitchen that I started writing *Spellbound*, although at the time I wanted to call it *War and Piece*. Thank you to Ethan Bassoff, again, for not letting me call my book *War and Piece*.

I want to give the biggest thank-you to the good people of Oshawa, Ontario, for being, collectively, my first audience. The Shwa boys and the toxic posse will always have a place in my heart and in my comedy. Shalom Harlow gave me an escape plan and shelter. One of the greatest things that ever happened to me was meeting my beloved Ronnie. I didn't know someone could instantly become family. Geoffery Milnes, Ryan Hamilton, Paul Bae, and Pugs always pick up when I call and tolerate me ordering a coffee mid-conversation. Mr. Armstrong helped me achieve what everyone said was impossible by spending endless hours with me in the Learning Resource Center. Thank you, Alan Madill, for your artistic expertise. David Flink gives me the opportunity to speak to and connect with other members of the neurodiversity community and lets me be a part of Eye to Eye. Thank you to Elizabeth for making me feel like the greatest writer in the world, even though I know I'm not even in the top three. And for making the lyrics to "Standing on the Moon" ring true.

Thank you to Robert Hunter and John Perry Barlow for teaching a kid who struggled to learn to read that words could take you on a journey. And to the Grateful Dead for teaching that same kid that the journey could be to a different galaxy.

About the Author

Phil Hanley is a proud dyslexic and an internationally touring comedian who has made countless TV appearances, including on *The Tonight Show Starring Jimmy Fallon*. He has recorded two comedy specials, *The Half Hour* for Comedy Central and *Ooh La La*, which can be found on his extremely popular YouTube channel. A passionate advocate for neurodiversity inclusion, Phil sits on the board of Eye to Eye, one of America's biggest nonprofits for neurodiverse students, and promotes neurodiversity acceptance in his viral stand-up videos and at in-person events across North America. He is a regular at the Comedy Cellar in New York City, where he lives. He'd hate for me to tell you this but he used to be a model.

tudders- stutters

inolige — analogy

Showin — shoe in   Dielsdorf - Düsse

paytrons

atractive —attractive

manspaning-

udaucie — audience

refultable — refutable   cost

incent — Innocent

u

realcannizing—recognizing   Adventag

perpetuly — p

ztep — stairs

Boardway   — Broadway   dylexicia

hussle — hustle

pupu

selfetreem — self esteam

i

conveustion-conversation

g

Tracked - entacted
in (tacked)

Cariline